Remote Work and Cheap RV Living

A solo woman's journey of working remote, traveling and living full-time in an RV while preparing for early retirement.

By Chris Conley aka RemoteChris.com

Remote Work and Cheap RV Living

A solo woman's journey of working remote, traveling and living full-time in an RV while preparing for early retirement.

By   Chris Conley

www.RemoteChris.com

Published by Chris Conley

Email: Chris@RemoteChris.com

Mailing address: 2657 Windmill Pkwy, #297, Henderson, NV 89074

Copyright 2019 by Chris Conley

All rights reserved. This book or any portion thereof may not be reproduced or used in any manner whatsoever without the express written permission of the publisher except for the use of brief quotations in a book review.

I decided to write this book to share my journey, experience and knowledge with others who may be considering working remote, buying an RV and hitting the open road or retiring early.

This is an opinion platform. The content is based on my experience and my journey. I encourage you to do your research before making any big life decisions. Other people's results will vary. Make your own decisions based on your own needs.

Follow the Blog at:

http://remotechris.com/

Follow RemoteChris on Facebook:

https://www.facebook.com/RemoteChris

See RemoteChris's unique designs on Funny T-shirts and Cool Coffee Mugs at:

https://whizzyshop.com/

Etsy: https://www.etsy.com/shop/WhizzyShop

Teespring: https://teespring.com/stores/whizzyshop

Amazon: https://www.amazon.com/s?k=whizzyshop&ref=nb_sb_noss_1

Social Media for WhizzyShop

Facebook: https://www.facebook.com/WhizzyShop/

Instagram: https://www.instagram.com/whizzyshop/

Twitter: https://twitter.com/WhizzyShop

Pinterest: https://www.pinterest.com/whizzyshop/

TABLE OF CONTENTS

SECTION ONE: An Introduction   PAGE 9

About Me

My Travel Beginnings

Make Time for Travel While You Are Healthy

SECTION TWO: Find a Remote Job   PAGE 15

The Number One Question I Get Asked: How Did I Land a Remote Job?

Remote Jobs, Work Camp and Local Jobs

Possible Remote Work While Living in an RV

Staying Connected with Internet While Working Remote From Your RV

I Retired at Age 55

Being Self Reliant and Grateful. An Attitude of Gratitude

SECTION THREE: How to Retire Early   PAGE 28

How to Retire Early: Introduction

My History; Things That Worked, Until They Didn't

How To Retire Early – Step One Review Your Monthly Expenses

My Thrifty Spending While Living in an RV

Pay Off All Debts Especially Credit Cards

Housing Expense

How Much To Save For Early Retirement

Ways to Earn Extra Money

SECTION FOUR: Find an RV   PAGE 40

Feeling the Need for Change – How It Began

Researching the RV Lifestyle

Sitting on the Fence, Not Quite Ready to Jump

What RV Should You Buy? Big or small?   Part One

What RV Should You Buy? Big or small?   Part two

What Works For Me; Keeping It Simple in My Small Class C

SECTION FIVE: Preparations Before Moving Into the RV   PAGE 55

Downsizing; Less Junk More Adventure

Insurance

How To Handle Mail While Living In Your RV -Mail Service and Residential Address

Getting To Know My New RV

Knowing Your RV Systems; Liquid Propane Gas (LP)

Knowing Your RV Systems: Electrical

Knowing Your RV Systems; Plumbing

Money for Maintenance and Unexpected Repairs

RV Life with Arthritis Hands or Other Physical Limitations - Part One

RV Life with Arthritis Hands or Other Physical Limitations - Part Two

Always Have a Back-up; Plan B

SECTION SIX: Informed Travel   PAGE 82

How to Decide Where to Travel; So Many Choices

Community, Socializing and Meeting People While Traveling

Is RV Life Safe for a Solo Woman and Aren't You Scared?

When Your Family and Friends Express Concerns About Your RV Life

Keeping a Travel Journal, Spending Log and Taking lots of Photos

How To Prepare For Travel Days

How To Decide Where To Travel; So Many Choices

Styles of Camping: RV Resorts, Campgrounds, Boondocking

Campground Memberships

All About How to Be Successful At Boondocking

Finding a Good Boondocking Location

Do You Need Solar To Boondock

Conserving Water When Boondocking

Where to Get Water, Dump Tanks and Trash While Boondocking

SECTION SEVEN: Budget and Expense   PAGE 105

Budget

My Actual Expenses for 3 Years

My Current Situation with Expenses

SECTION EIGHT: Travel Log   PAGE 111

Grand Canyon South Rim, One of My Favorites

Great History in Los Alamos, New Mexico

Aliens in Roswell, New Mexico and Hiking Carlsbad Caverns

SECTION ONE

An Introduction

About Me

Hi, I'm Chris. I am a solo woman living full-time in my RV. I work remote and travel around the country seeing new places. My life is about collecting experiences. I love learning new things, trying something different, exploring hobbies and having new adventures. I love my remote RV life. I look forward to sharing my journey with you. Below is a little of my recent history or her story:

Since the spring of 2017, I have lived, worked and traveled in my 19 ½ foot Class C Motorhome full-time. As a solo woman over age 55, this has had some unique challenges and provided a lot of great adventures.

I have worked entirely remote since December 2011, first from my house and then from my RV. The first seven years was working for corporations and then I retired from the corporate world the first week of 2019. At that time I took a year to rest, relax and recharge all while living and traveling in my little RV home.

I now work for myself, in an attempt to work fewer hours and have more flexibility in when I choose to work. At the beginning of 2020, I was ready to get back into some kind of work. But, it had to be working for myself, working much fewer hours and not having a set schedule. I wanted more of a hobby situation that might bring in a little income. So, I am now self-employed and developing a few different income streams. Growing a small business does take time and hard work, so it might be a few years before I start seeing any good results. That's OK, I'm patent.

I have a blogging website which is one of my hobbies. It is a way to share my adventures through my blog writing and sharing travel photos. It is also a way to answer people's questions about how to work remote, how to get a legitimate remote income while living and traveling in an RV and how to manage RV life as a solo woman.

I have a lot of various interests and therefore some of my blog writings might seem like they are all over the place. If I'm living it, I will write about it. I do try to stay away from drama, so I won't be talking about politics and religion in my posts. Also, I'm a Gemini, so I have that duality thing going on. Some days I'm this and some days I'm that. I'm a work in progress, so you won't be seeing the perfect life here; I'll share the good, the bad and the messy stuff too.

Continue reading as I go deeper into my journey, my early retirement, my remote work and my RV life and travels

My Travel Beginnings

Several years ago, thinking ahead to retirement, I was researching ways to live cheaply within the means of a small retirement check. I knew I would have to drastically cut back on spending, payoff all my credit card debt and somehow find super cheap housing without taking on a mortgage. I was trying to figure out a way to retire a few days before my 55th birthday. This became my new goal, which seemed impossible at the time because I had very little savings and no other assets.

At age 50, due to life circumstances, I was renting a house. I have owned homes in the past, but after the 2008 housing crises left me burnt out and stressed, I was not ready to take on a mortgage any time soon. I have always felt and still feel that the price of an average home in any decent city is just too high. I know most people consider it an investment, but after 2008, I just can't gamble like that.

So, anyhow, I was doing a lot of searching the internet on cheap living and came across people living full-time in their RVs, trailers, and vans. Then, I remembered having known a few people who retired and traveled in their RV or several people that moved to a senior RV park in south Florida.

This got me thinking that perhaps I should do this sooner than retirement, so that hopefully, I could live cheaper sooner and payoff my debt while I was still working a good paying job.

I researched RV travel for about 3 years before I bought my first RV. After owning the RV a few months and doing some short travels, I decided not to renew the lease on my rental. I started living in my RV in July of 2017. One reason was so that I could head south during the winter and find warmer weather.

This is something that I had dreamed of all my life, so finally at age 54, I was happy to be able to do this. But, another reason was to try to reduce my monthly housing cost. The high cost of rent was eating up most of my monthly income and it seemed to increase every year. The added benefit was that I could travel around the country, mostly in the summer time, and see places across the country that I had not seen before.

It is exciting for me to get up in the morning and look out my window, which has an ever changing view. Yet, I sleep in the same bed every night and I'm so happy to travel with my own bathroom and refrigerator. I have all of the comforts of home in my little motor home. I call it my studio apartment on wheels. When I'm in my RV, I feel like a turtle, safe in my little shell with everything I need.

Make Time for Travel While You Are Healthy

I have talked to many RVers who said that they had always wanted to travel in an RV and that they had talked about it with their spouse for years. Sadly, many of these RVers only made the move after their spouse had gotten sick and passed away, realizing too late that life is short and an extended life is not guaranteed. There are also hundreds of people that I have met online that want this lifestyle, but they are waiting for any number of things to happen or to finish before taking the leap. I hope they all have a chance to experience this lifestyle, even if it's only to rent an RV for a week during their vacation.

I have heard many stories of people dying or getting really sick just days or weeks before their scheduled retirement. This is so sad, when a person has not had the time or opportunity to follow their dreams.

None of us are guaranteed a tomorrow, so we must live for today. Even if you only get out on the weekends or a few weeks in the summer, I encourage you to get out there. Go for a walk in the park, go see that funny movie, take up bicycling or hiking or swimming at the local aqua center. Just get out there and get moving. Sitting in a chair all day, every day is not good for the body or the mind.

SECTION TWO

Find a Remote Job

The Number One Question I Get Asked:

How Did I Land a Remote Job?

Short answer is; years of various office experience along with some good luck or good Karma.

I have worked for the past 40 years. As a single mom, it was necessary that I work full-time and in order to be home evenings and weekends, office work seemed like the best way to work during the time my daughter was in school and to be home when she was not. A lot of that was working minimum wage or doing entry level office work. In 2001 I happened to get a job in the mortgage fulfillment industry. Over the years, I worked my butt off and was able to get promoted. At one point around 2007, the senior manager over my department gave us all laptops to work from home. The only rule was that we had to put in our 8 hours at the office first, Monday thru Friday (40 hours). OK, but we were salary and did not get paid for the extra work. LOL, well that was my second time working remote.

My first time working remote was when my daughter was about 3 years old and got sick, so my boss loaded the typewriter into my car expecting me to work with a sick kid at home. Yeah, I got nothing done. No surprise there. Good thing her illness was minor and I was back at the office within a few days.

My third time working remote was when I quit my job in 2011 to move out of state. It was hard having that conversation with my manager, but I chose to move to another state to help out family. A few hours later when the head honcho came in, he asked me into his office to see what he could do to keep me. I said nothing could keep me, I had made plans and that was that. He then asked me to work remote, so that I could keep working with the client I had been working with for the past 6 months. Of course, I happily said yes. This offer came with the stipulation that I would only be working when there was work to do and there were no benefits with this position. This kept me working part time from home for about 8 months. But, once the client project was finished, there was no more work for me. So, I began to search for a new job. Karma was with me, because I ended up landing a great full-time remote position. Read on.

So my most recent remote job (#4) was working full-time for a corporation. I got this job by answering a job ad for which I was qualified and had a lot of experience. I had several interviews over the phone and eventually passed a background check. I never had a face to face interview with anyone. I found this strange, since my new employer was a large worldwide bank. But, I guess due to my experience, they were happy to hire me sight unseen. Also there was that 90 day probation period for them to see if they liked my work. I guess they did, because at the end of 5 months I was given a huge bonus if I agreed to stay with them for a year. Um, heck yeah, I couldn't sign that contract fast enough for a bonus equal to 4 months pay.

This new job paid a regular paycheck with benefits. 40 hours a week, regular office hours, Monday thru Friday. I logged onto the computer at home and stayed in my seat diligently working, meeting production numbers and getting good evaluations on my quality. Of course, I worked in my pajamas some days, took showers during my break time, and at times threw a load in the washer or ran out to grab some food. Really I was way more productive working from home than I ever was working in an office, where there was always too much noise, too many interruptions, awful office politics and brushing off chatty Kathy's.

This job lasted more than 6 years. The best part was that the pay was equivalent to my team members who were working in the corporate office. I had no one looking over my shoulder, but I did have my manager and team members on instant messenger if I needed anything. IM also let my manager know when my computer was active or not. LOL, so there is no cheating when working remote. If you go this route, know that you do have to put in the time, meet product and quality numbers and actively participate just like being in the corporate office.

During my time there, I knew my entire team was working with one client and that the corporation that I worked for had a contract with that client. Well sometime in 2018, during a meeting, my boss said that the contract was once again up for renewal and under negotiation. Then some weeks later they let us know that the contact would not be renewed and that we would finish up current files and then be out of a job. Eventually work slowed down to a trickle and I got the layoff call the first few days of January 2019. The corporation put my status as "retired". Well, I guess I reached my goal of retiring at 55. The only constant is change.

I was rather happy about being laid off. I was more than ready to take a break from working. Up to that point I had worked consistently for 38 years, with just a few months off in the year 2000. I was really looking forward to taking at least a year off. Of course the layoff came with some severance money to cushion the fall and I was eligible for unemployment after about 8 months, which helped. I also had a little savings which was good for my mental outlook to keep me from having anxiety, although since I was living in my RV, my expenses were already pretty low. I at least did not have to worry about a mortgage or other heavy debts.

People ask me all the time to tell them who I worked for, but I can't say. I will not divulge my past employers name nor the clients I worked with. I signed multiple non-disclosures over the years, so I don't talk about specifics.

So, that is my history on how I started working remote. My advice; ugh, why did it take me 3 minutes to try to remember that word, friggin senior moment. Anyway….

My advice to someone looking for a remote corporate job would be to look at what your current job is and see if you can do that remotely. Or look at your skill set and see if that will fit into any remote work. Lastly, perhaps learn a new skill. IT work seems to have a lot of positions out there with the opportunity to work remote. There are also a lot of companies that have remote Customer Service workers, if you don't mind being on the phone all day. Good luck.

Remote Jobs, Work Camp and Local Jobs

Most full-time RVers are retirement age and receive some sort of retirement income. Many folks have put their time in, working 35 to 50 years and putting money in savings for their retirement years. This leaves them free to travel and explore without concern for a monthly income. But sometimes, the retirement income is not enough and they decide to supplement with a part time job or a camp host job.

On the other hand, younger people, who have no savings, find other work to fund this lifestyle. Some people will stay in an area for several months and work a local job or campground job, and other people are lucky enough to find remote work that they can do from their RV while parked anywhere.

In whatever town you land in, there may be seasonal work or places that are looking to hire someone just for a month while the tourists are in town. There are camp host jobs available at a lot of the campgrounds and RV parks that you see around town.

Temp Agencies: Maybe you just want to work in the winter and travel in the summer. Or perhaps you need a short term temporary job to cover some unexpected repairs. There are temp agencies that can place you somewhere for a few weeks or few months or whatever you are looking for. Some temp agencies are nationwide and therefore, when you get to a new town, you may already be in their system.

Below is a sample of options that can get you thinking about how you might fund your full-time RV travel adventures. This list is just a starting point, to get you thinking about what you might want to research on your own.

Possible Remote Work While Living in an RV

Corporate Jobs:

Travel nurses usually work 6 week to 3 months in one area and then move on to the next job

IT tech jobs seem to have a lot of remote opportunities

Call center jobs that can be done remote with phone service over the web

RateRaceRebellion.com is a site that posts legitimate remote work opportunities. Lots of call center customer service type jobs

Teaching English to Chinese Children thru the internet seems to be a popular way for RVers to earn money

Fiver.com might work for you as there are lots of legitimate posts seeking a variety of skills; graphic design, secretarial, bookkeeping, data entry, writing and other skills

Start Your Own Business or Side Gig:

Fiver and other web based job connect sites, for small jobs to do if you are just looking for a few extra bucks. Although some of these can turn into long term full time gigs.

Sell something online, such as essential oils, vitamins, or jewelry that you make

Offer services to fellow RVers, such as RV washing, solar installation or engine maintenance.

Side gigs; mowing lawns, dog walking, babysitting, sewing or house cleaning.

Sign up with a Temp agency to do weekend work or whatever you can find to fit around your current work schedule.

Staying Connected with Internet

While Working Remote From Your RV

Most people these days like to stay connected to family, friends and work, even while traveling and camping. This is easy to do as long as you have a decent cell signal. Going to remote areas and having cell service can depend on your phone service carrier. The majority of RVers find Verizon works even in remote areas. Other people find ATT&T covers them sufficiently. I've talked to some RVers that work remote and they insist on having two carriers, so that they have a better chance of being able to connect for work, no matter where they are.

Before going full-time, I bought a Verizon Mifi and added it to my cell plane for an extra $20 a month. This works as a wifi hotspot to provided wireless internet within the range of your RV or campsite. Verizon calls my plan unlimited, but for the Mifi, they may slow down the connection after I reach or exceed 15 GB in a month.

I find 15 GB is more than enough for the work I do, even when I use to be on the laptop 8 hours a day connected to my former employer. If I do go over the 15 GB, I have not noticed a slow down. However, there have been a few areas that have been slow due to a lot of people accessing the same tower. This can be an issue when you are in a seasonal spot, such as snowbird locations in winter or cooler mountain locations in summer.

Streaming TV; When I went full time in my RV I added a tablet to my cell phone plan for an extra $20 a month of unlimited data. I find this works well for streaming TV shows from Netflix and other streaming services. It seems truly unlimited as I have never noticed a slow down even when using 30 GB or more in a month. I can also use the tablet as an extra hotspot if needed. I also noticed that in some locations, the tablet gets a better cell signal than the Mifi or my cell phone, and so I sometimes use it to connect for work. For some reason, different products can get a better or worse signal, I assume, based on their internal antenna or other components.

Cell Booster: A cell booster is a device that will take a small cell signal and boost it, so that you can get a slightly better signal. These come with a very small antenna and you might be better off to buy a larger antennae that can reach farther away. Also keep in mind, this only works if there is an existing cell signal. If there is no signal at all, this device will not help you. I have one of these and it has come in handy a few times to keep me logged in to work. I bought the weBoost for about $500 in 2017. I don't think it has been worth the money. I find it easier to just move to a location that has a better signal.

Wifi Booster: This device will pick up a wifi signal, like from McDonalds or the campground and give it a slight boost. This can get rather complicated because you have to load the software onto your computer and if the wifi requires a guest login, then there is that extra step. You can find further information on line. I have one of these, but I rarely use it. I bought the Wifi Ranger for around $350. I don't think it has been worth the money as most wifi signals are not strong enough to do what I need, so I prefer a cell signal.

Campground Wifi: It has been my experience that campground provided wifi is usually extremely weak, if you can even get a signal. Do not expect a decent campground wifi signal to get you connected for work, you will be disappointed. If you need to be connected for work, make sure you have your own equipment.

Free wifi locations: There has been a few times over the years when I needed to sit at McDonald's parking lot, coffee shop or a hotel room and use their wifi for work. This is part of always having a back-up plan and being prepared to switch gears to get it done.

Old School Entertainment: DVD player and books and hobbies; During those times when I absolutely can't get a wifi signal, I make sure that my back-up plan is old school for entertainment. I bought a small TV with a built in DVD player. I buy used DVDs from thrift stores. I like to get complete seasons of TV shows on DVD. I also love to read, so I keep plenty of used books on hand that I get from the thrift store or from various campground libraries where you can leave a book and take a book. I also keep a small amount of paint supplies and craft supplies. There are also other hobbies that can be done from the RV. Find what works for you.

I Retired at Age 55

In early January of 2019, the corporation that I worked for laid off a bunch of people, including myself. They officially put me into "retirement" status. This was good news to me as I was ready for a much needed break and It came with a nice severance package.

I was more than ready to have some time off, as I had been working without a substantial break for almost 40 years. The good news is that since I had been living in the RV for over 2 years, I was prepared. I knew that my monthly expenses were low enough that I could not only survive but I could thrive with this new direction my life had taken. Perhaps if it had happened 5 years ago, I would have been devastated with no way to pay my monthly debt and other living expenses.

Since my full-time RV living is cheap, I had already paid off all my debt and I had put money into savings. I plan to live extremely cheap to make this money last as long as possible.

I'm sure after some time off, I will want to find a hobby that I can somehow turn into a little side money. I may even work part time for a non-profit, working remote from the RV of course or who knows what the future holds. The great thing is that with my expenses being so cheap, I have options. I have options that I would not have had 5 years ago living in a house.

I have tried all variations of this RV lifestyle and I am confident that I can continue to find very cheap ways to live to make my savings last longer.

Being Self Reliant and Grateful. An Attitude of Gratitude

If you decide to move into an RV full-time and travel, you will be better off with the attitude of being self reliant. You won't always have someone around to fix every little problem. It helps to have the right mind set. I find it very empowering to try to tackle issues on my own first and it is very rewarding when I can accomplish something on my own. If you have the money, you can always hire the help you need. But, this really is no different from living in a house or apartment. Shit happens and you deal with it.

It also helps to keep a spirit of adventure. When you find yourself in a new town or a deserted forest road, look at it as a grand adventure. Look around, notice the nice scenery and be thankful that you get to experience something new. I call it an attitude of gratitude. It is wonderful to get to experience so many different places, climates, landscapes, and cultures.

For more travel log, journey stories, and remote working ideas, check out my blog at RemoteChris.com.

SECTION THREE

How to Retire Early

How to Retire Early: Introduction

Early retirement is a dream many people have. Retirement is something that should be planned for decades in advance. It is something most people start saving for at a young age. Unfortunately I was not able to save for retirement until I was almost 40. But, I have found a way to work around that little problem. I will share with you this information in the coming chapters.

The RV lifestyle is intriguing to a lot of people. Living in an RV full-time and traveling can be a very rewarding experience. Doing it solo, has its own set of challenges, but nothing too hard. I have found that living full-time in my RV has enabled me to live moderately cheap. I've been able to payoff credit card debt and put extra savings into the bank.

I have been traveling and living full-time in my RV, as a solo woman, since early 2017. I love being able to explore new areas and beautiful scenery. I absolutely love sleeping with the window open and seeing the stars twinkling on a dark moonless night. The slightly cool breeze coming in through the ceiling vent brings in fresh air for a good night's sleep. I sleep much better out in nature, cozy in the RV, than I ever slept in a house or apartment.

There is nothing that tastes better than having dinner cooked over a campfire, even if that dinner is simple hotdogs and foil roasted potatoes. I love sitting outside in the sun with a good book or hiking a beautiful path in the forest or desert.

I decided to write this book to share my journey, experience and knowledge with others who may be considering buying an RV and hitting the open road and retiring early.

This is an opinion platform. The content is based on my experience and my journey. I encourage you to do your research before making any big life decisions. Other people's results will vary. Make your own decisions based on your own needs.

My History; Things That Worked, Until They Didn't

Over the years I have lived in a lot of rented apartments and rented houses and I have, at times, owned houses that were heavily mortgaged. In some cases, I moved because the neighborhood turned yucky, or I just wanted more closet space or a better school district. You know how it goes, it worked for a while and then it no longer worked for me.

With every mortgage, it always seemed that the mortgage payment was a hardship and at a larger amount then what I was really comfortable with. Usually the mortgage payment ended up being twice what the local rent was. But, I kept telling myself it was an investment. I mean, this is what adults do, right, buy a house and pay it off before retirement. In my case, I would have been paying for 30 years and not paying it off until age 75. Ugh …. I was still trying to figure it all out.

Some of my homes, I have sold for a profit and I thought that would always be the case. Boy, was I wrong. The last home I owned was a victim to the 2008 housing bubble crash and I was left with a mortgage that was double what the property was worth. I was stuck in that house for several years beyond what I wanted. I got to the point where I really needed to move to another state to be helpful and supportive to a family member. I was ready to just walk away from the house. Finally the bank agreed to a short sale and I was able to move. This has left me a bit shell shocked. It might be a long time before I'm ready to take on another mortgage.

I tended to move around every 2 years. It seems I always got restless and wanted a new neighborhood or a new layout and plenty of times I moved to a totally new state. I even moved cross county several times in my life, the most memorable being 4 cross country moves in 23 months during 2012/2013. But, it started long before that, at the young age of 19 when I made my first cross county move from the Midwest to the warm south. I guess I was jealous of the snow birds and decided to become one at the age of

19. A snowbird is a term used to describe people who live in the north and go south for the warmer winters.

Each and every time I moved cross country, I had to decide if paying for a rental truck or moving company was worth the cost. Each time I decided that it made more sense to sell my used furniture, have a garage sale and just buy new or used when I got to my destination. I could replace my furniture and other items for less than the cost of the rental truck and the huge amount of gas it would take for the truck to go a thousand miles.

So with each move, I only took what would fit in my car and sold or donated the rest. I don't regret any of it. Each of those moves was a fresh new start and an exciting adventure. But, of course, it can be costly to buy new stuff each time, even if it is used thrift store stuff. But hey, I like shopping for stuff.

Now, with living in the RV, I move as much as I want and everything I own is in my RV. Maybe someday I'll buy another house, but I will always keep the RV for some adventures.

How To Retire Early – Step One Review Your Monthly Expenses

The first step to being able to retire early is to be able to know what you are spending your money on and stop foolish spending on a bunch of stuff that you don't need. It is time to recognize your spending habits. If you want to retire early, you have to first of all, get a handle on your expenses. Stop spending so much money every month.

To begin, take a very close look at your bank statements and credit card statements. Circle the items that are things that are frivolous and that don't really serve a good purpose. Now total up these amounts, so that you know how much you spend a month on unnecessary things. Also circle all the times that you eat out or grab drive thru and total up the amount of money you spent on that. Now, review all of these statements every month to keep a check on your spending and also to verify that there are no fraudulent charges.

Most Americans spend quite a bit of their money on eating out at restaurants. There is nothing wrong with this, just make sure you are aware of how much you spend. Maybe consider cutting back to twice a week and find places that are less expensive but still satisfy your taste buds.

Once you are aware of the items that you are spending good money on, that don't really serve you or that you consider to be just draining your wallet, then you can make the conscious decision to avoid making these bad purchase choices in the future.

Before considering how to retire early, I was spending way too much money on my two week vacation every year. I spent a lot of money on plane tickets, hotel rooms and cruise ships. I still do this a little bit, but I am now way more frugal about it and don't do it as often. I can travel cheaply in my RV and still get the great satisfaction of having a vacation.

I honestly feel that life should be about collecting experiences. It would not be much of a life if you just stay home and never go anywhere or do anything. So spend a little here and there, but be mindful of it. Find free or less expensive places to go, like local parks or zoos. I find that going to city and state parks can be a great relaxing and fulfilling experience.

Another item you need to be aware of is monthly subscriptions that you signed up for but perhaps no longer use. These often go unnoticed on credit card statements. Make a list of all of the monthly subscriptions that you have. These will have shown up on your bank and credit card statements when you review them. You may have things like; cable, internet, gym and other memberships, newspaper or email subscriptions, Netflix and other streaming services.

Go thru your list and cancel the things that you no longer use or that no longer brings you joy. I found that I could easily live without cable and broadband and just use my phone service for internet and streaming Netflix. I was also able to cut out a few streaming TV services that I no longer used, as well as some subscriptions that I had forgot I was paying for.

My Thrifty Spending While Living in an RV

One thing that is important to keep in mind, is how not to spend money. Living in the RV with its very tiny space, means that I cannot just buy whatever I want. I have to consider where it will fit in the RV. If I buy a new shirt, I will probably have to give an old one away to Goodwill. This is how it works for buying a new towel, book or frying pan. So, with this in mind, I really spend far, far less, than I did in the old days of living in a house or apartment.

I also eat at home more often now. When I was working in a corporate office, I would stop and buy my coffee and breakfast sandwich on the way to work, and also pick up lunch and dinner the same way. When I worked remote from home, most days I would drive to some place for lunch, as it was just easier than cooking for myself. It could be very expensive when looking at the monthly total. I think this was my way of rewarding me for working 8 hours a day. Now eating at home, I save a bunch of money, eat healthier and I have lost a few pounds as well.

Living in the RV, I eat out maybe once a week and I really don't spend much money at all. This might be because I am happier living in the RV and perhaps I'm not trying to find happiness through shopping or eating out. There is a saying on the internet, "I don't need therapy, I just need to go camping". LOL

One other way that I save money is to buy my DVDs and books from a used book store or thrift shop, or better yet I use the free book exchange at the campground or RV park. I'm not spending money on mortgage, large appliances, big ticket household repairs, and no more of those expensive vacations.

Fun cheap RV living and frugal spending, means that with any money that I do make, I have some left over to put into savings.

Pay Off All Debts Especially Credit Cards

If you want to retire early, it is required that you stop all unnecessary spending. Absolutely stop using credit cards and stop going into further debt. Stop putting anything on the credit card and pay with cash or debit card. Completely stop adding to your personal debt. Unless you have a zero interest card that you pay off in full every single month you should not be using your credit card at all. Credit card balances have a way of growing all on their own. You want to keep those cards paid off for good.

The extra money you save spending this way should now be used to pay off all debt; largest interest rate first. Make a list of your debts, car loan, personal loans and credit cards. Now look at each statement and write down the current balance as well as the interest rate that you are paying. Make a note of the most recent month's interest amount you paid on each account. When you add up the actual amount of interest you paid in one month, you may be shocked.

Once you have your list, make it a priority to pay off the credit card with the highest interest rate first. These days it is not surprising to see that you might be paying 15% or more in interest on a credit card, maybe even as high as 21%. That would be over $50 a month on a $3,000 balance and that $50 could have been sitting in savings for retirement. It will take some time, but be diligent about paying down these credit cards every month and not adding anymore debt to them. Try to pay for everything with your debit card or with cash.

Car note and student loans are considered to be OK debts. These are usually lower interest rates and therefore they don't need to be the focus until the credit cards are paid off. Mortgages are usually not considered part of the items that you need to payoff. If your interest rate is a mere 4% or 5%, it makes sense to not pay it down when you have other debts to be paid off first.

Housing Expense

Take a look at your housing expenses and consider if this could be lowered. If you have a mortgage, can you lower the interest rate or payment amount? If you rent, can you move to a cheaper place such as going to a smaller apartment? Can you try to use less electricity or gas? Can you cut the TV cable service, broadband or house phone?

Do some research and consider moving into a situation that will be a less expensive monthly housing cost. There are two reasons for this; one is so that you can live cheaper right now and pay down debt and then once debt is paid off you can put money into savings. The second reason for this, is so that you can practice how to live cheaper because once you are finally able to retire, you will want to live as cheaply as possible or as cheaply as is comfortable for you.

Roommate: Maybe consider renting out a room in your house or apartment. Or do the opposite and you rent a room from a friend or family member. This way your monthly housing is cheaper and you have the added benefit of having the company of other people.

In one former house I lived in, I was able to offer temporary rooms to rent thru Airbnb. I did this for a while and made some extra money that came in handy to pay down my debts. Airbnb is an online place to match people offering a room for rent with people who are looking for a place to stay. At the time I lived in a tourist town, so this worked well for me.

My first step in lowering my housing cost was to move out of a rented house and into an apartment. This cut my monthly housing bill in half. I knew it would only be for one year while I continued my RV research. Long before I was able to retire, I followed my personal choice and moved into my RV. This works because I try to find places to park it that was cheaper than the rent I was paying.

How Much To Save For Early Retirement

Savings is key to early retirement. Put every extra dime into the bank. Keep yourself motivated by having reminders of your goal. Put a picture on your refrigerator of something that represents retirement for you. Put a note on your bathroom mirror of what your goal is. Stay dedicated to not spending and to putting money into savings.

Keep track of every penny that you spend. Month after month, review your expenses and remind yourself of what you could have done without. At the end of 12 months, you will have a better idea of how much money you need to live on. We will refer to this as your Total Cheap Monthly Spending amount. This will come in handy when trying to figure out how much money you need to save for retirement.

Go to the Social Security Administration website and see how much money you will get if you retire at 62, or whatever the earliest age is that you are allowed to collect Social Security retirement. Once you have this number, let's say its $1,500, then you can compare this number to the number that you call your Total Cheap Monthly Spending amount. If your SS retirement amount is less than your monthly spending amount, then you have some work to do. You either need to cut more expenses or save a lot more money for retirement.

On the other hand, if your SS retirement is a lot more than your monthly spending amount, then you may be able to use money in your savings account to retire early. If your monthly spending is $1,000 and you have $20,000 saved, you could potentially retire 20 months early. Of course you will not want to deplete your savings entirely as you will still need an emergency fund.

Ways to Earn Extra Money

If you find that you have already cut back on expenses and still can barely cover your bills with your current paycheck, you may need to consider some ways to earn extra income.

Perhaps consider going through your belongings and see if there is anything that you might be able to sell at a garage sell or on a local selling app like Facebook and Craigslist. Look thru your garage, attic and basement and see if there are items that are no longer used.

Maybe consider making some extra cash by mowing lawns, dog walking, babysitting or house cleaning. Sign up with a Temp agency to do weekend work or whatever you can find to fit around your current work schedule.

Consider some part time online work such as thru RatRaceRebellion.com or Fiver.com. If you have secretarial skills, graphic design, bookkeeping or data entry skills, this might work for you. There are lots of legitimate companies that will hire customer service people to work from home. If you don't mind being on the phone and can commit to being available certain hours, this might work for you.

SECTION FOUR

Find an RV

Feeling the Need for Change – How It Began

Several years ago, after I turned 50, I was living in a rented house and wondering how I was ever going to be able to afford to retire. It seemed like every paycheck went for rent and credit card bills with very little money left over to save for retirement.

Looking at the amount of Social Security retirement income I would receive, once I reached retirement age, I knew there was no way I could live off that, if I maintained my current spending. Especially knowing rent would just keep going up every year.

I was spending a lot on airplane tickets and hotel rooms for those 2 weeks a year that I could take a vacation from work. I was shopping and buying stuff I didn't need. I was trying to put money into a retirement plan, but it wasn't much, as I was trying hard to pay off the credit card debt. I knew I needed to get a handle on the spending and find a much cheaper way to vacation.

So, I was trying to figure out a way to live cheaply in the future, after age 62 or 65, when I would eventually take my Social Security retirement. Somehow I stumbled upon RV living and I remember a few co-workers from my past had chosen this path. This sounded intriguing, but I didn't know anything about it and knew that I had to do a lot of research before making any decisions.

The more I thought about living in an RV and traveling, it started to feel like I should do it sooner than age 62. I thought maybe I could figure out a way to do it within a year. My new goal was to get into an RV, live cheaper and payoff my debt. This would have the bonus of being able to travel cheaply as well. I was already working remote from home, so my income would continue while living in an RV.

So my research began.

Researching the RV Lifestyle

I researched everything on RVs. I delved into learning about the different types of RVs, the different styles of campgrounds and RV parks. I explored and researched the different working systems of an RV. I went to a lot of RV shows to walk through the many different types of Motorhomes and trailers. This kept me busy while trying to find the right RV situation for me.

I rented Airbnb RVs to get a feel for living in the small space and experiencing the RV systems. One was a small Motorhome and one was a slightly larger trailer. These were stationary, so I never actually drove an RV until I bought one. But I did enjoy those small rented spaces and it gave me the experience I was looking for.

While researching, I realized that I didn't want to tow a trailer and I didn't want to tow a car. I was sure that I wanted a Motorhome that would also be my daily driver. So, I was looking for something small that would fit into a regular parking space. I thought the van style Class B would be perfect. However, these are very pricy and I felt like this was not an affordable option for me. I started leaning in the direction of a smaller Class C.

I knew I wanted a vehicle that I could stand up in. I wanted something simple, minimal tires, no slides, no automatic jacks, and no automatic stairs. I knew the more simple the design, the less potential for things to go wrong. Less moving parts meant fewer things to maintain and/or fix. I knew I wanted lots of windows to let in the sun in the morning and the stars at night. I wanted the basics of a shower, toilet, fridge, stove, heater and air conditioner. I also needed at least 4 seatbelts available for days when family would be joining me. My list was long, but it kept me focused in my search.

The last thing I wanted was to spend thousands of dollars on a vehicle that would not work for me in the long run.

I researched every style of RV and trailer and even looked into van conversions. I researched all of the different systems in an RV, to see how they worked and what could potentially make them stop working. I really did a lot of research to see if I wanted to do my own van conversion. I quickly realized that since I had never done any home renovations and was not a carpenter or plumber or electrician, that this would be a project too big for me. So, although I think I could do the design portion, I didn't feel that I could actually cut a board or have the physical strength required to fit the pieces together.

After all of this I had a pretty good idea of the style of RV to look for. Next I had to turn my attention and research to other logistics of the RV lifestyle, like how to get mail and how to maintain consistent internet for my remote job while traveling to different states. I was also well aware that I was living in a house surrounded by furniture and a lot of "stuff" that would not fit into a small RV.

Sitting on the Fence, Not Quite Ready to Jump

Part of my research was trying to figure out if living in an RV could actually be cheaper. I knew it would largely depend on finding places to camp that were low cost. I was starting to do a lot of research about boondocking, which is camping for free, often with no hook-ups, sometimes referred to as dry camping. This seemed exciting and yet moving into the unknown. I have always just plugged into the house electric with no issue and flushed the toilet without thinking about where it all goes. The longest I had been without city electric was a few hours at most, during a severe storm. Living off grid in an RV seemed like an exciting challenge.

I was renting a house at the time with combined rent/utilities of approximately $1,400 or more a month. I also had a car payment on a new car that was basically just used to drive to the grocery store. As I was already working from home, I didn't need a car to drive to work every day. So a car payment and car insurance was another expense that I could probably have lived without.

Once my house lease was up, I was still afraid to take the plunge of moving into an RV. I was nervous about the unknown. Also, I was not quite convinced that I could always have an internet connection for my remote job, if I was traveling in an RV. I felt like I needed a little more time.

I took out a one year lease on a small apartment, which was about half the cost of what I was paying to rent the house. I sold my furniture and down sized as much as possible. At this time, I knew I would eventually move into an RV, but I also knew that if it didn't work out or if I didn't like it, I could just go back to renting an apartment.

I had the bare essentials in this little apartment. I slept on a cot and had a futon for a couch. I kept everything boxed up and only unpacked what I needed. For instance, for the kitchen, I basically had one frying pan, one coffee cup and I used paper plates. During the 12 months in that apartment, I learned what few items I really used and over time got rid of things I did not use.

During this time, I also experimented with different ways to connect to the internet without using the broadband cable service I had. I bought the Verizon Mifi and drove around to different locations to test it out. I also added a tablet to my phone plan, so that I could stream Netflix and Hulu.

I had given up watching cable 2 years before and found streaming much more enjoyable, as I could watch what I wanted, when I wanted with no commercials, and it was much cheaper than cable. Adding a Roku device or Amazon Firestick to my TV's was an easy way to get my favorite TV shows. Ditching the cable was one thing that I could easily do to save money on my monthly expenses

During my research time, I paid close attention to what mail I was getting. I made sure to choose paperless on all my bills. It turns out that 99% of my mail was junk that went straight to the trash. Other than the new bank card that comes every 3 years, there was really nothing important.

A few months before moving into the RV, I got a digital mail box. This is a service that throws out junk mail and scans other mail. I can go online or on my phone to see the image of the envelope received. They will scan the contents at my request. They will forward select mail items to me at an RV park or General Delivery upon my request. As for a primary address for the DMV, I use a relative's address, although Escapees can also be used as a primary address.

I had already been working remote, at home, for 4 or 5 years, so working from the RV was just a matter of making sure I always had a good internet connection. For this I made sure to have Verizon, which seems to have the best coverage in remote areas.

What RV Should You Buy? Big or small?   Part One

Motorhome or Trailer? Class A, Class C, Luxury Van, Small Trailer or Big Fifth Wheel? So many options. If you are one of the thousands of dreamers that are considering the RV lifestyle, then I'm sure you already know that you will need to do your research before taking the plunge and buying one. Research is essential to see what kind of RV is right for you, as well as what size. There are a lot of options to choose from; Motorhomes, trailers, campers and vans, which all come in various sizes and lengths.

Some things to consider when trying to decide, is how often you will be moving the RV, along with how big the RV or trailer is. If you plan on doing a lot of traveling and if you think you'll be in a different spot every 2 or 3 weeks, you might want to consider something smaller, easier to maneuver. I feel that the more you move around, the smaller your RV should be. If you plan to move a lot, then a smaller Class C, truck camper or small trailer might be best for you.

If you think you will only move seasonally and will be parked in the same spot for 4 to 6 months, than a much longer RV won't seem like such a hassle when you are only moving it 2 or 3 times a year. Moving a 40 foot fifth wheel trailer every other week, might be stressful, well, at least it would be for me.

Of course, you also need to consider how many people and pets will be using the living space. A family of 4 with 3 pets will need a much larger space than a solo person with no pets. So, if you have kids and large dogs, you may want something with plenty of room to spread out.

Do you want to tow a trailer with a truck? Do you want to tow a car behind a Motorhome? Are you comfortable with hitching and unhitching? Are you comfortable with driving down the road with 15 feet of truck and 30 feet of trailer? Do you want a smaller Motorhome with a Moped on its rear rack, or maybe a camper truck that will be your daily driver?

Make a list of the amenities you think you want. Some things to consider: Plenty of head space to stand up and move around, separate shower, called a dry bath or a smaller wet bath where the toilet is in the shower, an oven, a microwave, heater, air conditioner, the size or capacity of your hot water heater, the capacity of your fresh water tank, grey and black tanks, ceiling vents and fans, how many electrical outlets and 12 volt outlets, how much inside storage room and outside storage room. This is just a small list to start you on your own research of possible amenities.

Do you want to have easy access to go from bed to driver seat, or have access to the bed, toilet or fridge while on a road trip? Keep this in mind when looking at Motorhomes with slides, as some RVs with slides pulled in, block access to the toilet or fridge. Also keep in mind that with a truck camper or trailer you will have to exit the truck in order to gain access to the living area; bed, toilet and fridge. Will you be comfortable doing this when parked at a roadside rest area or when spending an overnight at a Walmart or casino parking lot?

For safety reasons, a lot of women feel more comfortable when they are able to pull over to use their own private toilet without having to exit the vehicle. There is also comfort in knowing that if you would ever need to leave your site in the middle of the night, you can simply go from the bed to the driver's seat all while having the safety and security of being locked inside your RV.

What RV Should You Buy? Big or small?   Part Two

I have heard that a lot of people buy their first RV and then within a year or two, they are buying something else, either bigger or smaller. So, renting before you buy might save you from this very thing.

I would advise you to try out several Motorhomes and trailers to see how they feel to you. Also, keep in mind that although a large part of your day may be spent enjoying the outdoors, the inside space does matter. I knew I would be working inside 8 hours a day, so that was a consideration when I was shopping for an RV. Also there are rainy days, humid evenings and cold mornings where you may be more comfortable inside your tiny living space.

There are some YouTube channels that will take you on tours of various sizes and types of RVs, trailers, campers and vans. Bob Wells YouTube channel is one example, that has a lot of these types of videos and it may be helpful to you. Some dealerships also will have YouTube videos that take you on a tour of different RVs and explain their amenities.

You can go to dealerships and RV shows to do a walkthrough of many different styles and types of RVs. It is a good idea to walk thru as many different styles as you can. Even if you think you want something big, look at the smaller ones and even if you think you want something small, walk thru some of the bigger ones.

Don't leave out any options, as it doesn't hurt to look and educate yourself on what is available. Even if something is way beyond your price range, go ahead and walk thru it, because down the road, you might find an older used one that is similar and within your price range.

It may be a good idea to rent a camping trailer or RV Motorhome on Airbnb or a similar website. This way you can move into the RV for the weekend or the week and get a good feel for what the tiny living space is like and also familiarize yourself with the difference in how the RV systems work.

There are also companies where you can rent a Motorhome, camper truck or van and drive to some campgrounds or cross country to really get the full RV experience. This will go a long way in helping you decide how big or how small you want to go.

While you are doing your research, you might try moving into the smallest room in your house and see how you feel just hanging out in that small space. Make sure that room has windows and make yourself a comfy couch or daybed with all of your favorite hobbies and Netflix. This will simulate what it is like to hang out in your RV on a cold or rainy day. This might also get you thinking about what items you would want in your RV and what items you can live without.

Now once you think you know what RV you want and how big or how small, the next step is deciding if you want something brand new, slightly used or very old. The price will vary greatly depending on the type and age of the RV.

When shopping for an RV, just beware of scams. When buying from a private owner, take precautions and if it sounds too good to be true it probably is. Never send money orders thru the mail as a deposit, this is a red flag for a scam. Do your research and be aware. Good luck.

RVs come in many different sizes and styles. Here is a list to help get you familiar with the different kinds used and the different ways that people camp. This is just a beginner list to help you get started on your research.

Class A; bus style Motorhome

Class B; van style Motorhome

Class C; truck front style Motorhome

Truck camper

Small trailer

Fifth wheel trailer

School Bus converted to an RV

Box Truck converted to an RV

Van conversation with a bed and portable toilet in your van

Car camping with a bed in your car and maybe a cook stove set up outside

Tent camping out of your car

What Works For Me; Keeping It Simple in My Small Class C

As a solo woman with no pets, I found the RV that works best for me is a small Class C. This is a Motorhome with the truck front and overhead cab area. It is easy to drive, easy to back into a site and does great on the road. I am very comfortable living in the tiny space and it is a perfect size for my mode of RV life, which is moving around every couple of weeks.

When doing research, I thought I wanted the van style Class B, but these were just too expense for me. I also didn't want something 20 years old; because I knew the consistent, costly repairs would be a headache for me. I wanted to keep it very simple. For me, that meant no slides, no extra moving parts and no extra gadgets. No extras meant fewer things that could break or need maintenance. I was worried that if I had too many hassles to deal with in the first six months, then I would quickly go back to living in an apartment.

The slightly used, small Class C works for me because there are no slides, no dual tires, no electric stairs and no jacks. I bought it 4 years old, but the trade off was high mileage. I was gambling that I wanted a newer updated living space and probably would not be driving that much to put too many more miles on the engine. I had also read that a lot of RV parks don't want RVs over 10 years old. At the time, I didn't know if this rule would impact my ability to find places to camp.

For me, keeping it simple and basic means I don't want the hassle of towing a trailer or a car. No hitching and unhitching. The RV I found is just very basic and simple with no extra frills. My RV has a wet bath and no oven, but other than that, it still has all of the conveniences of a small home. When I'm at the grocery store, I fit into a regular parking spot and have the convenience of putting my new groceries straight into the fridge.

I like the handiness of going from the driver seat to the living area without exiting the vehicle. On a road trip I can pull into a roadside rest and use my own private bathroom in the safety of my own home. I can also make coffee, get something cold from the fridge, make a sandwich or lounge on my couch for a rest, and easily get back to the driver's seat without going outside.

I like the small Class C, as I don't want to mess with a tow car, so it serves as my daily driver. RV Park set up is basically pulling into an RV spot and plugging in the electric cord. I only dump the tanks every 3 weeks or so and at the same time I fill up the fresh water tank. I never keep hooked up to water at the RV site, as I don't find it necessary. So set up takes one minute, just plugging in electric. When I want to go explore tourist stuff or go to the store, I just unplug the electric cord and drive off. Keeping it simple for me is the key to loving this lifestyle and minimizing headaches.

SECTION FIVE

Preparations Before Moving Into the RV

Downsizing; Less Junk More Adventure

This step can be very time consuming, so I suggest you get started as soon as possible. It may take you several months to go through all of your belongings and whittle it down to what will fit into an RV.

Some people also find this process very emotional. It can create a lot of anxiety. You will have moments of doubt and asking yourself if you are doing the right thing. Just keep your goals in mind and remind yourself why you made the decision to get into the RV lifestyle.

I have moved cross county so many times, that I am an expert at downsizing. I will try to share some helpful tips with you. I suggest doing the following, several times in stages. If you have 5 years of stuff or 50 years of stuff, it will take weeks or even months to go thru this process.

First off, go room by room and pick out stuff that is easy to sell or give away. You know if you don't use it and have not used it in 6 to 12 months that should be an easy decision. Be real, you don't need 3 irons, 4 crock pots, 98 shirts and so on.

Next go back thru each room and have a pile to keep, a pile to trash, a pile to sell, a pile to donate. This step you can do each week or each month and get that keep pile smaller and smaller. Everybody I know takes way more clothes and dishes with them in the RV then they need. I myself, go thru my things every few months and donate the items I find I don't use.

Take your books to the used books store for cash. Give the rest to a thrift store. Sell your kitchen appliances on eBay or have several garage sales. Remember, you don't want all that junk to keep you from your RV adventures.

Buy a cheap scanner and scan all your important documents and photos and put them on small SIM cards. If you must keep some photos, make the pile very small. Give them to your relatives to keep for you.

Collectables and memorabilia can be hard to give up. There will be items that you won't want to part with for sentimental reason. I had a huge collection of refrigerator magnets from my travels. I ended up taking digital pictures of them. Now I can look at the digital pics and I don't miss those magnets at all. I did keep two coffee mugs that I had bought on vacation and I find 3 years later that I don't use them. I can now donate them to a thrift store.

I have heard of people who attach a lot of sentimental value to items that belonged to relatives who have passed. These can be the hardest things to let go of. Try keeping a digital picture of the item and passing the item on to a relative or donating to someone who can use the item. Your loved ones who have passed would not want you to miss out on your RV adventures because you are hanging on to too much stuff. Read that last sentence again until it sinks in.

Some full-time RVers find peace of mind by putting some things into a storage unit. But, they also discover that after paying storage fees for a year or two, they are no longer attached to the items and find it easy to give them away. You will have to find your own way thru this.

Some RVers put furniture and everything into storage and pay it for five years, knowing eventually they will move into a house or apartment. Everyone has to make up their own minds based on their financial and other goals.

Insurance

I'm not going to talk much about the different types of insurance that you will need to live full-time in your RV; because I'm sure you are all adults and know this already. I'm no expert so here are the basics:

Liability and Collision: You need liability insurance in order to drive a vehicle. You will want collision insurance if your car, truck or van has a value higher than what you are comfortable covering on your own. You will also want insurance for your RV Motorhome or trailer for the same reasons.

Roadside Insurance: Roadside assistance insurance for me is a must have. This has come in handy to get someone to change my tire on the side of the road or help me when I get locked out. It also covers towing if you have a break down and need to get towed to a repair shop.

Health Insurance: I would think that most people already have health insurance either thru their retirement or thru their employer or even if you are self employed you have bought your own health insurance. If you currently don't have health insurance, you can do your own research online, talk to an insurance agent or go to healthcare.gov.

But I just want to say a little bit here that nationwide health insurance might be hard to get. Not too many places offer it. Even if your insurance is only good in your local area or state, most insurance will at least cover emergency services while out of state. Always check with your insurance provider for details.

As with any lifestyle, you will want to have insurance to cover those unexpected occurrences in life.

How To Handle Mail While Living In Your RV –

Mail Service and Residential Address

A mail service is a great way to deal with mail while you are on the road. I don't have an actual physical address, no house or apartment, as I am traveling and staying in different locations and different states every week or two. I find that having a mail service to deal with my mail is worth the money, so that I don't have to deal with it or worry about it.

Of course, you will want to have all of your accounts set to paperless, so that actual paper is not mailed out to you. This option is available with most bank accounts as well as just about any place that you do business. Accessing your accounts online is the practical way to go when living and traveling in your RV. Going paperless is necessary, as this will reduce your paper mail as much as possible, and you want all of your accounts accessible online, so that you don't have a bunch of paper taking up room in your RV.

There are many places where you can have your mail sent. Some people use a UPS store mail box, which will give you a street address and they will receive your mail. You can contact them periodically for them to forward your mail to you at your RV site or to General Delivery in the town you are staying in.

Most towns have one or more post office locations where you can pick up mail sent General Delivery. I have my mail sent to me about once a month to General Delivery. This has worked great and I have been able to receive my mail in several locations throughout my travels.

One thing to keep in mind is that General Delivery will not accept a UPS package. When ordering from Amazon or some other online store, you can request USPS to be sent general delivery or you can request UPS and have it sent to your RV site. Another great option is Amazon locker, which is available in some towns.

Another option is to receive a large envelope containing your mail at your RV site if the RV park allows package delivery. Check with your RV park to see if this is allowed and see if they have a handling charge. Some places charge $2 or $5. Some UPS stores will also receive a package for you for a fee, but as each business is run individually, you will have to call them to find out the details.

Another option is having a digital mail service that will scan your envelopes and contents so that you can view it from wherever you are and see your mail on your laptop or on your phone screen. These companies will also forward whatever mail you desire to your location upon your request. I have this service and find that my mail is very minimal. Most mail items I receive, I can look at the scanned contents and then have them put the paper in the recycle bin. This way it is not necessary for them to forward the mail.

Due to the Patriot Act that was passed after 9/11, most banks require a physical residential street address. Some DMV offices do as well, especially when applying for the updated drivers' licenses that are Real ID compliant. I think the idea behind the law is so that they can locate your physical person if needed.

For an actual street address, I find it easier to use a relative's address, just for the DMV and bank. But even with these, I also give them my mailing address, so that any actual mail goes to the digital mail service. If you don't have a friend or relative's address to use, you can use Escapees Texas or other mail services for a physical address. Escapees Texas works because they also have an RV park, so that it does not bring up a red flag and does not show as just a postal mail box service when giving your address to a bank.

Keep in mind that the residential address you give the DMV should be in the state where you declare residency. Some states have no tax on a person's income and therefore may be a better option. Currently the no income tax states are Alaska, Florida, Nevada, South Dakota, Texas, Washington, and Wyoming

There are some You-Tube videos out there showing how someone will rent an RV site for 30 days and use that address for their physical address. This can be tricky but it seems to work for some full timers. When they leave the RV site, they just continue to use the address, which of course only works when you use your mailbox mailing address to get your mail.

I have tried 4 different services over the years. A general mailbox is good for receiving items of less importance like magazines, annual camping passes and other membership type mail. For the more important stuff, that you would want to see right away, I love having the mail scanning service. If you get an important notice from your bank, or government office, like jury duty notice or other government notice, you can read the scanned document usually right on your phone.

If you are still in the research phase and still in a house or apartment, this is a good time to start going paperless with all your accounts. It is also a good time to start using a mail service, so that you can see how it works and see what mail you are getting.

Getting To Know My New RV

After my extensive research I finally decided a small Class C RV would work for me. These were hard to come by and it took me many months to find one. During this time, I continued to watch You-Tube videos of other full timers and make my preparations.

I eventually found the right RV for me. I bought it while still living in an apartment, which meant I had to pay monthly fees to store it, since large vehicles was prohibited at my apartment complex.

So, once I bought the RV, set up mail service, sold or donated my stuff and bought the equipment I thought I needed, I moved into the RV and began my adventures.

When I picked up the RV, the sales guy walked me around the outside and the inside, explaining how to use everything and how it all worked. Luckily most of this made sense, as I had been watching a lot of YouTube videos that had explained this. I knew that the only way to learn more than I already knew was by experiencing it firsthand.

Driving the RV off the dealer lot was the first time I had ever driven an RV, or any large vehicle. I went very slowly, checked my mirrors constantly and found a route that would take me thru the least traveled parts of town. I went directly to my apartment and got the items I thought I would need for a weekend. Then I went to a nice RV park to spend the weekend getting use to the RV and learning how to use each system. I also didn't want to drive too far away from the dealership in case there was something that needed their attention.

During that weekend, I made a long list of items that I thought I needed; tea kettle, can opener, an extra throw pillow and some paper cups, etc. The next weekend, I invited the two grandkids to hang out with me. I made sure to spend a lot of time outside, as my RV is too small to have active young kids bouncing around and leaving their clutter everywhere. But, we passed the test and still liked each other at the end of the weekend.

For the next month, I took weekend trips, going further away each time. Then I did a whole week and then a whole month several hundred miles away. I loved it. I loved every minute of it. I was relieved to know that it was not a mistake giving my 60 day notice at my apartment. When the day came to give up the apartment key and move into the RV, I had no regrets.

Knowing Your RV Systems; Liquid Propane Gas (LP)

An RV has different appliances and systems, just like a house. It is a good idea to familiarize yourself with the RV systems. You may have to do occasional cleaning, maintenance or repair on these systems.

Most all RVs have the following systems that run on propane; oven, stove, hot water heater, furnace and refrigerator. I find that I need to refill my 10 gallon propane tank about every 6 weeks when dry camping or every3 months when plugged into electric. However this will vary for other RVers who camp in very cold places or have other heavy uses.

My propane tank is installed onboard so I have to drive the RV to a place to get it refilled. Most large U-haul dealers can do this. I usually just Google "propane near me" and get some ideas on where to go.

The RV refrigerator will run on propane and use a small amount of 12 volt electric for the fan. In addition, I use a little fan placed inside the fridge, operated by two D batteries. This circulates the air, which helps keep it cooler. The fridge can either run on propane when dry camping or run on electric when the RV is plugged in. Keep in mind that the fridge has to be kept level in order to run efficiently. If it is off level for too long, it may cause issues, break components and not run properly.

If your fridge stops getting cold, you can get a bag of ice to put in it. Keep the fridge door closed as much as possible. No need to buy a cooler as the fridge is much better insulated. This should get you by until you can get the fridge fixed. Before calling a repair man I usually Google the symptoms and try to figure out if I can get it running on my own. However, I've had the mobile RV repair service come to my campsite to make repairs that were beyond my abilities and that time I needed a few expensive new parts.

I love my little propane two burner stove top in my RV. I use it every day to boil water for coffee and tea. My stove is the type where you have to turn on the gas and hold a lighter to it for it to get a flame. So, I find it handy to keep a long handled lighter slid thru the drawer handle beneath the stove. My RV does not have an oven, so I cannot comment as to how they work. I never used an oven much in my house so I don't miss it, not being in the RV.

Most RVs have a small 6 gallon hot water heater. I never use it and keep it turned off all the time. I have gotten use to washing my hands in cold water. Most people find that they only turn their hot water heater on as needed about 20 minutes before they plan to shower or wash dishes. I don't use my RV shower due to the small space, I prefer the campground shower. I just don't feel that I need the hot water heater and haven't for the 3 years I've been living in my Class C Motorhome. When I first got the RV, I did test the hot water heater and the shower, just to make sure they worked.

If I want warm water for my Waterpik, or to wash dishes, I just heat some water on the stove in a kettle. It is much faster than waiting for the hot water heater to heat up and uses less propane, as it is heating less than half a gallon of water, as opposed to the whole 6 gallons in the hot water heater.

RVs are set up with small circular vents on the back of propane heaters and refrigerators to allow air flow into the RV from the outside. I always keep my kitchen ceiling vent open an inch or more, to let clean air in and keep the oxygen level up in the RV. Even on the coldest nights, I will leave it open a slit.

I find that I don't like to use the propane heater during the night, mostly due to the smell of propane. I might turn it on early in the morning when I wake up. Instead, if I am plugged into electric, I use a little portable electric heater, set at the 700 watt setting. I find this is more than enough to heat up my little space. I make sure to keep rugs and other objects well away from the heat source.

Caution; never use an extension cord with any appliance that has a heating component as most extension cords will overheat and can cause a fire hazard. Always plug directly into the outlet. I make sure to keep the batteries in both smoke detectors up to date, just one more thing to not worry about so that I get a good night's sleep.

RVs are equipped with a hard wired LP gas detector. These can be sensitive to other odors such as perfumes, cleaning sprays and even dog farts. So, if you find yours going off, check to make sure Darling Doggie isn't lying right next to it.

Keep in mind that the built in LP gas detector will go a little crazy at when it is about 5 years old. It will go off like it is low on batteries. A reset will work the first few times, but at some point, usually in the middle of the night, it will go off and not stop.

Yes, this happened to me. I stopped mine by taking out the fuse that goes to the LP gas detector. That night I found myself driving to a motel at midnight. I wanted to be safe because at that point, I wasn't comfortable sleeping in the RV with no working LP detector. The next morning I went to Lowes and bought a portable one that is good for LP, carbon monoxide and smoke.

This is another example of being flexible, having a plan B and fixing things for yourself. At some point, I might pay to have the hard wired one replaced.

Knowing Your RV Systems: Electrical

Most RV Motorhomes or trailers have the ability to plug into either 30 amp or 50 amp. An RV with two ceiling air conditioners will probably require a 50 amp hook-up. My small Class C is 30 amps, but I keep an adapter on hand, in case my assigned RV spot is 50 amps. Keep in mind that when you plug into the campground electric, you might hear your converter come on for a few minutes. It is a small humming sound. This device takes the 110/120 and converts it to 12 volt for some of your house systems, such as the water pump and house lights. The 12 volt system will vary according to what type and brand of Motorhome or trailer that you have.

In my Class C, the house/coach battery, 12 volt, will keep the fridge fan working on the propane setting, and allow me to use the water pump, propane furnace and lights. However if I want to use the electrical outlets, microwave or air conditioner, I have to plug the RV into a 30 amp receptacle or turn on the generator. Your RV will have sensors to tell you when your house/coach battery is full or low.

Some RVs have 100 to 400 watts of solar on the roof. Keep in mind that although this will be plenty to run a laptop and small devices, even possibly a refrigerator, this will not be enough to run the AC, microwave, hair dryer or electric heater. If you plan on dry camping and need to use these appliances, you'll need to use your generator.

Most RVs have an air conditioner and a microwave. These two items use a lot of electricity, so the RV will need to be plugged into your generator or plugged into shore power in order to use them. 100 to 400 watts of solar will not be nearly enough to run these major electric hogs. My small electric heater is 700 or 1,200 watts, my AC is 3,500 watts and my microwave is 1,000 watts. That would take an enormous amount of solar panels and battery bank to run these items. Shore power is the term used when plugged into electricity at a campground or RV park, usually at a 30 amp or 50 amp electrical post.

I don't like running the AC. It is too loud and the air coming out is too cold for my small space. I have always been the type to have my windows open for fresh air. So, when planning where I am going to stay, I really try to find spots that are going to be mid 70s during the day and 50s to 60s at night. This is my happy medium. Of course I still end up in places that reach over 100 degrees in summer and have cold nights plunging into the 40s or lower. But, that's OK, if I get really uncomfortable, I can drive to a different climate.

I have a 400 watt inverter plugged into the truck dash (12 volt cigarette lighter) to charge devices while driving or boondocking (dry camping). Boondocking or dry camping is a term used when you are camping with no hook-ups to electric, water and sewer. The inverter turns 12 volt into 110/120 and some also have USB charging outlets. If you decide to get a dash inverter, keep an eye on it, as it may drain your engine battery when using it while parked. I keep a small meter handy that plugs into the cigarette lighter, to tell me if my truck battery is getting low.

I also have a few portable generators, which are large lithium batteries that I can use to plug in the laptop, TV, and other devices. I've also used these to power up a personal size blender and a Waterpik. These batteries can be recharged by plugging into electrical or dash 12 volt or using a solar panel. The solar panel comes in handy while boondocking or dry camping.

My Class C has several back-up options that will keep me going if one of the batteries fails. If the truck battery gets drained, there is a switch on the dash that allows me to start the motor from the house battery. If the house battery fails, I can plug into electric or start the -generator to get it charged again. It also charges when the truck engine is running, like while driving. I also have a small solar panel on the roof, a trickle charger that slowly tops off the house battery when the sun hits it. This small solar panel was enough to keep my propane fridge fan running while I was away on a cruise for 8 days, even in Seattle where it is not always sunny.

Some Motorhomes come with a built in generator that are directly connected to the gas tank. This comes with a failsafe that will not let the generator work if the gas tank goes below ¼ tank, so you are not stranded with no gas in your tank. Most trailers do not come with generators.

I rarely use my generator, but I make sure to start it at least once a month and use it for 30 to 60 minutes. This is necessary to keep the gasoline from settling and causing issues with deposits. The generator needs routine oil changes and maintenance, just like any other engine.

I use rechargeable batteries as much as possible. Energizer brand works great for me. I keep a variety of small batteries on hand for little devices such as; flashlights, smoke detector, fans, etc.

Knowing Your RV Systems; Plumbing

Plumbing items in the RV consist of toilet, shower, sinks, hot water heater, fresh water tank, grey tank and black tank.

RVs have two options for water source. You can run water from your fresh water tank or from a hose connected from your RV inlet to a campsite water hook-up. Since my RV is my daily driver, I find it easier to just use water from my fresh water tank and not keep the hose hooked up to the campsite. This way, when I come and go every day, I'm just unplugging the electric and I'm ready to go. Easy peasy.

RVs come with fresh water tanks to hold water that you can use for showers and cleaning dishes, etc. The size of the tank will vary from 15 gallons to 60 gallons. If you are dry camping, you will learn quickly how to conserve water so that you don't need to find a refill station every other day. In order to use water from the fresh water tank you need to flip the switch to turn on the water pump. As this gets its power from the house battery, it is best to only turn this on when needed and turn it off when you are done.

I never drink from the fresh water tank. I use gallons of bottled water for drinking and making coffee. Some people use a good filter system. It is also necessary to sanitize the tank as often as necessary so that even hand washing can be done without fear of getting sick. Every 6 to 12 months I will sanitize the fresh water tank by pouring a cup of bleach in my 20 gallon tank and fill the rest with water. I wait 24 hours, drive around a little and then drain it, fill it with fresh water and drain it again, to get all of the bleach water out. If I lived where it is humid all the time, I would probably sanitize much more often.

The kitchen sink and shower will drain into a grey tank and the toilet will empty into a black tank. The size of these tanks will vary and can be large or small depending on your rig. Mine is 17 gallons but most larger rigs have 40 gallon holding capacity.

Your RV will have sensors to tell you when your tanks are full, low or empty. Keep in mind that your black tank sensor will rarely work correctly. Once you get a bit of goo on the sensor it will always indicate the tank is full, even when it is empty. If you allow food particles to go down your kitchen sink, you may have the same issue with your grey tank.

I usually use my fresh water tank sensor to let me know if the black and grey tanks are getting full. If the fresh water tank is getting low, I know that the water has gone into the grey and black tanks, and therefore is a good indicator of them getting full.

When the black tank is at full capacity, I can tell because the waste will be clearly visible coming up the tube to the toilet. When the grey tank overflows, it overflows into the shower floor. I have been doing this long enough to know that I can go more than 3 weeks and still not have full black and grey tanks. So, I make sure to empty them every 2 to 3 weeks. You will, in time, get to know your systems and how often they need dumped and filled.

Toilet; You may have a time when your toilet flush lever breaks and the stinky stuff is sitting in the toilet bowl. When your lever breaks and no longer opens the little trap door to let the bowl empty, you have a problem.

Yes, this happened to me. Of course I had to get that toilet bowl empty manually, not only for the smell, but before calling a repair man to come to my site. I had to get out a Dixie cup and scoop out the nasty stuff into a trash bag, then wipe the bowl with paper towels and a vinegar water solution. I was able to use the campground bathroom until I could get my toilet fixed. Some people use the bucket method, but luckily I did not have to.

Money for Maintenance and Unexpected Repairs

Anytime you own a house or a vehicle, there are things that will need to be maintained on a regular basis and things that will need to be repaired. Some of these you can do yourself and others will need to be done by a professional. You will need those regular oil changes and the normal maintenance that goes along with having an engine.

You should have a monthly budget for normal wear and tear items and an emergency fund for big repairs. You will have issues with tires that need replaced on a regular basis. We have all had that nail in the tire, or the big bulge, at some point in our travels. This is something to consider when you are looking at a small Class C with 4 tires or larger vehicles with dual tires. How many tires do you want to maintain?

I seem to get a rock in my windshield every year or so. This may happen to you also and when it does, the windshield needs to be repaired or even replaced. A Class C truck windshield can cost $200 installed and a large Class A windshield can cost $2,000 installed. Keep this in mind when researching the type of RV you want to purchase.

You will also have some wear and tear on the household items and appliances. Don't be surprised when you have 3 cabinet latches that get broken the first year out or blinds that need to be replaced within a matter of months. I've been replacing my broken cabinet latches with the child safety kind, just because they are easier for me to install.

Then there are the more costly items that may need attention, such as a toilet flush handle that breaks or a fridge that no longer gets cold and needs a new circuit board.

Luckily there are many problems that you can troubleshoot yourself with the help of Google and YouTube. I find it very empowering to find that I can fix something all by myself and with just a $2 item from Home Depot.

RV Life with Arthritis Hands

or Other Physical Limitations - Part One

Being over age 55, I've had arthritis pain and joint pain for a few years now. I find this can cause limitations especially in the use of my hands, wrists and thumbs. I am just not able to grasp an object and turn it or twist it or anything else that requires even a little bit of muscle use. I'm also not able to carry objects palm up. For instance, I can't carry a coffee mug more than a few feet and I can never carry a tray or a stack of folders. For some reason, my muscles just fail me or it is too painful. So, I have to find ways to adapt and get on with my day. Here are a few examples of how I found ways to adapt when it came to RV related issues.

Dumping tanks: After living in my RV for 6 months, I had a problem with sewage leaking out the side of the sewer drain hose when it was supposedly twisted into place on the RV for dumping. This was probably due to a worn out gasket or it may have been because I could not twist it tight enough. The sewer hose was hard for me to screw on and screw off. It was exhausting dealing with it and I found myself not dumping very often because I could not deal with that sewer hose.

I also had a very embarrassing incident, when one time I did not get the sewer drain hose on tight enough, due to my hand limitations. When I released the black tank, the hose came off the RV and the black tank contents aka poo, spilled all over the ground, all over my shoes and splashed up my legs. This happened at a gas station dump site, where I was very visible, at the corner of a very busy intersection.

I was so extremely embarrassed to have 15 gallons of brown yuck covering the ground. My own brown yuck, that I prefer to keep a secret and pretend does not exist. That was not fun hosing that muck into the drain. I'm sure it only took a few minutes, but it seemed much longer. Oh, I can laugh at it now, but you know, at the time, it was not a good moment. Yes, RV life is always perfect, shiny and glorious. Not!

The solution was that I ended up buying a higher quality sewer hose and that seemed to fix both issues. After that, I didn't have the leak and screwing the new sewer hose on was easier, although it does take my combined strength of using two hands, at least it is doable for me. I am fortunate that I only have to dump every 2 to 3 weeks, so I can wait do it on a day when my hands feel better.

I also bought a new sewer cap that has a handle going horizontal across the cap, so now I just turn the handle and don't have to grip and twist around the circular cap. This $6 item made such a huge difference for my arthritic hands. Oh, I was one happy camper the day I found that item at the local camping supply store.

RV Life with Arthritis Hands

or Other Physical Limitations - Part Two

Water hose issues: Another area where the arthritis was causing issues was gripping the water hose to unscrew it from the spigot. Once I had to get a campground worker to come and unscrew the hose for me. This is hard for me, because I like to do things for myself. I now use a rubber gripper, which seems to help a lot. Another trick I learned is to turn off the water, squeeze the hose nozzle to let air pass thru, allowing the excess water to run out of the hose. This relieves the pressure inside the hose and makes it easier to twist the hose off the spigot. Now if I could just figure out a way to open the pickle jar or my jar of peanut butter.

My hiking stick aka walking cane: I always make sure to take my hiking stick with me when hiking in unfamiliar places. Some uneven terrain can result in a slip and fall or a twisted ankle. The hiking stick is a great way to prevent unwanted accidents and injuries. It's also a little security knowing if a coyote gets too close, I have something to waive in the air as I shoo him off. But that never happens; coyotes only want little dogs and bunnies. LOL

I have even used my handy hiking stick a few times when my hip arthritis is acting up or one of my knees decides to go a little wonky on me. I don't let it stop me, I still need to go out and run errands or walk to the hot tub. Of course when these things flare up, I still go to the gym, but I avoid working those inflamed areas, feeling it better to let them rest and heal. Gosh, I hate looking like an old cripple lady, but some days that is exactly what I am.

Stepping stool: Another handy thing to have around is a small foldable stepping stool. This I use when cleaning the windows from the outside or getting to the back of the top shelf in the kitchen cabinet. Some people use a small stool in front of the RV stairs, if the first step is too high. You may have to think of some ways to get around your own physical limitations.

What are your limitations? When researching the type of RV you want, keep in mind your own limitations in relation to the design of the RV you are considering. Does the bathroom have a step up, are the RV stairs higher off the ground than you're comfortable with. Can you easily reach the outside connections for sewer and other outside components? If there are issues with any of these items, what is your Plan B?

Always Have a Back-up; Plan B

Whether you are nomadic or static, aka stationary, RV life is not much different from sticks and bricks life, when it comes to plans going sideways or something throwing a wrench in your works.

In every aspect of life, don't be surprised when something does not work or does not work out. Always have an alternate plan. Always have a Plan B and a Plan C. You will have things happen that delay your arrival time at the campground. Your toilet or fridge, at some point, will have issues and you may not be able to use it when needed. You will, at some point, land somewhere, such as a camp site that you prepaid in full, and find that there is no cell service and no wifi signal and therefore you can't connect to work. What is your Plan B?

I find it helps to be flexible. It also makes a big difference when you have an overall attitude of gratitude. You will have set backs, this is all part of the experience. You will have a greater appreciation for the good days, after making it thru a few not so good days. And hey, no matter if you live in a house or RV, sometimes things go a little haywire and we just have to deal with it.

For example, when I was planning a cross country trip in the RV, I knew I would be going thru places that I had never traveled or had not traveled in years. I had a loose idea of the route I would take and I had planned to avoid large inner cities, like Dallas. I knew I had to be flexible, take my time and not get anxious when things came up. Once I got near Dallas, I stopped for breakfast to wait for the early morning traffic to clear, knowing that in some cities, traffic could be an all day thing.

I was surprised to find out, last minute, that my planned route turned into a toll route. I immediately exited the freeway, pulled over and reviewed my options. I then found a route that took me around the southern end of the city and avoided the toll. And oh, what a lovely drive that turned out to be, unexpectedly nice.

Another example of having an alternate plan is when I am on a road trip and just need a place to park for one night with no hook-ups. I never know if I will only want to drive 2 hours or 5 hours in a day, so, I try to make of list of potential places I can park overnight along the route. Sometimes when I get to a place, overnight parking is no longer allowed or the neighborhood does not look safe. So, this may result in having to drive another hour. It's all about being flexible.

My first year of traveling in the RV, I had several instances where there was unexpectedly no cell signal when I reached my camp site. This was not good, as back then I was an hourly employee and required to sign into work during normal business hours. So, there was several times when I had to get up extra early and drive until I could get a cell signal. This is especially hard in remote mountain areas. I now know how to do better research and planning, not just using Verizon coverage maps, but I also use Compendium.com to check reviews which include information about how strong a cell signal is at a campground.

Don't get locked out of your RV. I've heard countless stories of people getting locked out of their RV under many different circumstances. For some reason, some RV doors lock automatically when they are shut. This has caused many curse words to be uttered when just stepping out of the RV to let the dog out or to check your clearance when backing into a spot. Have a Plan B.

Many people keep a spare key in their purse or wallet as well as another key somewhere around the RV. Keep this in mind, when planning your adventures. I've trained myself to never leave the RV without a key, even if I am just taking out the trash. However, there has still been a few times when I needed that spare key tucked inside my purse. I've come out of the grocery store more than once, only to realize I didn't grab the key before locking the door. Sh*t happens.

If you do get locked out, your roadside insurance should be able to send someone to your rig to help you.

For more check out my blog at RemoteChris.com.

SECTION SIX

Informed Travel

How to Decide Where to Travel; So Many Choices

I often say that I haven't been everywhere, but it's on my list. I love the experience of going to a new place and exploring everything about it.

Some people have asked me how I determine where I want to travel. This seems to be especially confusing for someone that wants to go everywhere and do everything. So, yes, the first year out in your RV, you might find yourself covering a lot of territory and moving/traveling every other day. This is normal and most people don't tend to slow down until after that first year or two.

The way I determine where I want to travel, is I basically think about where I haven't been and where I want to go. Once I have a few choices on my list, I look to see what time of year is the best for traveling to that particular destination. The weather is a big factor in my decision. I find that I don't want to be cold and I don't want to be hot. I prefer not to have to run the air conditioner or heater. That means I head south in the winter and north in the summer, or at least to a higher elevation in the summer.

I also tend to travel a lot further in the summer, putting several thousand miles on the RV and then returning to the south for the winter. In the winter, I tend to stay in one spot for 2 or 3 weeks and then not move too far to the next spot. Winter is more about resting, relaxing and recharging. This might also be the time when I work a little more to earn gas money for summer. Bonus if I can lay out in the sun in January. I love my RV life.

In the summer I do a lot more site seeing and going to places I have never been. Mostly because I want to see places up north, but I will only go during the summer months as I prefer to avoid snow and cold weather.

Some people like to do Route 66 from one end to the other. Some like to go visit relatives in other states. Some like to do a loop of the National Parks. Some just start heading in a direction and stop at places that look interesting.

Some people will plan every minute of their route and know exactly where they are going to stay and have reservations many months in advance. While plenty of other people just make it up as they go along. If they like an area, they stay longer. They may show up with no reservation or call it in a few hours before arriving. There is no right or wrong way to do this.

Some people make the rookie mistake of planning a trip and are surprised when they find themselves in snow in May, because they didn't realize that they would be at 6,000 feet elevation and did not check the weather for that month, in the area, when doing their research. Other people find themselves baking in 120 degree weather in Death Valley in the summer, due to it being at sea level. Yes folks, sea level can hot in the summer time and mildly warm in the winter time.

High elevations are cold in the winter time and mildly warm in the summer time. I like to research the average weather for the month when I will be traveling through an area and check the elevation. I find that 7,000 feet elevation is fine for me, but going 8,000 or higher, I tend to have a harder time breathing, which makes hiking no fun. These are things to keep in mind.

Community, Socializing and Meeting People While Traveling

If you decide to move into your RV full-time and travel, there is no need to be concerned about how you might go about meeting new people. Keep in mind that no matter where you go, there are plenty of opportunities to meet likeminded fellow RV enthusiasts.

When at a campground or RV Park you can meet people while out taking a walk, standing around the dog park or hanging out at the pool. There will be plenty to talk about as you are all there to enjoy the RV lifestyle and have that in common. Most RV parks and campgrounds also offer games and entertainment at the club house, which is a great opportunity to meet people. Some RV parks even serve meals at the clubhouse, where you can get some yummy food and get to know your new neighbors.

If you are out in the wild boondocking, meeting people may be a bit more challenging, but it can be done. While out for a walk or a hike, waive to your fellow campers and sometimes you'll get a waive in return. Keep in mind that a lot of boondockers like there solitude and go out to the middle of nowhere for the express purpose of being alone.

It has been my experience that most RVers are perfectly fine hanging out by themselves and most are not the type to get lonely. If you don't know what Introvert means, you might want to research it. A large number of solo RVers are Introverts and actually like having their alone time.

Keep in mind that some people may not be receptive to talking or meeting neighbors, especially if they work from their RV and just want to relax after work. So, if you find your neighbors not interested, or he or she doesn't act as friendly as you expect, that's OK too. With this lifestyle, we each can be as sociable as we feel like on any given day.

Is RV Life Safe for a Solo Woman and Aren't You Scared?

For some people, especially women, and solo women in particular, safety is a question that comes up a lot. Many people considering the RV full-time lifestyle have no experience with camping or RVing, so the unknown brings up some fears for them. Safety in an RV or at a campground is similar to living in a house, also known as sticks and bricks.

A big question that people ask; Is it safe traveling and living in an RV full-time? It has been my experience that it is just as safe as living in an apartment or house. It is just as safe as driving your car to the grocery store or to the next town. In either case, use the same precautions. Keep your doors locked for your own peace of mind. Be aware of your surroundings when you are outside. If you get to a campsite and it just doesn't feel right, move along, follow your intuition or gut instinct. I've only had this come up once or twice since I moved into the RV in early 2017. I just didn't have a good feeling, so I switched to plan B and moved on down the road.

When traveling, I like the Class C because I can pull into a roadside rest area and I don't have to exit the vehicle in order to use the bathroom, get to the fridge, make a sandwich, or rest on the couch. This gives me a much greater sense of security.

Some people are more comfortable traveling with a dog, as it can be your first alert system. Just keep in mind that traveling with a pet adds another layer of work and concern. You will have to consider what to do with your pets while you go into the grocery store or are out all day doing tourist stuff. Some RV parks won't let you leave your dogs outside unattended and have rules about leaving your dogs inside while you are gone due to barking or other concerns.

I don't have any pets, so I don't have any advice on the subject. But, that for me is just another layer of keeping it simple and having less responsibility. When I want to go on an all day train ride or a week long cruise, I don't have to worry about boarding a pet. But, we all have to find what works best for ourselves and our lifestyle choices.

For a feeling of personal safety, another solo RVer I talked to, keeps some items on the bedside table to feel more secure while sleeping. She has her key fob with the alarm button, a whistle and a hiking stick with the pointed end. She also takes these items hiking, to potentially scare off any predators such as coyotes. This might give you some ideas on how you can sleep easier, whether in the RV, a hotel room or your house. Some people prefer more lethal items of personal safety, so just remember; whatever you use in your home will also work in the RV.

In my 3 years of travel, I have not had any incidents where I felt directly threatened. I've been thru some sketchy areas and seen plenty of sketchy people, but not too much that raised my hackles, if you know what I mean.

I did have one night when I was boondocking in a forest and there was a family that was arguing late at night. They were far from me, but voices carry in the night. I turned on a fan to block out the noise and continued to try to enjoy the dark starry night, In that particular situation I did not feel threatened and I did not feel the need to move.

One other time, while at a campground in Tennessee, there was a couple having a domestic dispute, which involved shouting very loudly and gunning their car engine. At one point I thought I was going to be a witness to one of them killing the other. Really, they both were terribly aggressive and hateful to each other. I decided I had to get away from the negative energy and I really did not want to have to stick around to be a witness for a court date if one of them was injured or murdered. I seriously did not want to witness anymore of their bad behavior. And yes the woman was as bad as the man, they were equally matched in their bad behavior.

Luckily this campground had a lower section and an upper section. I was in the lower section because it was pretty much empty and quiet and down by the river. Once I decided to move, it was as simple as unplugging the electric cord and driving to the upper section. That is the only time I can remember moving once I was settled in for the evening. Also, that is the only time that things felt so uncomfortable that I had to move. One time in 3 years is not bad. I've had worse things happen in some apartment complexes I've lived in, where I could do nothing more than lock my door and hope nobody bothered me.

I did move campsites one time because the people next to me had a kid that liked to scream every 10 minutes because he didn't get this way. Oh, that is what I love about my home having wheels; I can just easily drive away and off to a better place.

When Your Family and Friends Express Concerns

About Your New Plan for an RV Life

During my research phase and the two to three years it took me to find the right RV, I did tell friends that I was shopping for an RV. I may not have mentioned my intention to move into the RV. I felt that until I actually made the move, this omission was just a matter of not speaking of something that might not happen. I was not fishing for any negative feedback while I was still just in the thinking about it phase.

Once I made the move into my RV, I explained that it might only be for a month and then I might consider getting an apartment. This was true because I knew that if there were too many maintenance issues or road mishaps that I would throw in the towel.

Although once I was in the RV, family and friends were supportive. I'm a solo woman and I have always taken care of myself. So, as I've never been dependent on someone else, my track record shows that I would not be asking for help from anyone.

But sadly, I have heard lots of stories where other people who are considering the full-time RV life, have been given a hard time from one or two friends or family members. When this happens, I can only advise that you to let friends or family members know that you have done your research and that you have a backup plan.

The negative reaction from people in your life could be coming from a place of fear, maybe because they have never camped themselves and are afraid for your safety. Maybe they are afraid you will run out of money and be asking them for help. Try to figure out what their concerns are and let them know what your research has shown and tell them of your many back up plans.

If you do tell your friends and family and then end up getting some negative feedback, perhaps it would be sparing their emotions to just not say anything until the deed is done. As someone once told me," their opinions don't pay my bills". Once you're living the RV life, you can send them picture of the fabulous places you get to visit. I have found that after moving into the RV and posting pics on Facebook, several friends are also now considering the RV life.

Keeping a Travel Journal, Spending Log and Taking Lots of Photos

I like to keep a travel log of all of the beautiful places and towns that I have the privilege of visiting and playing tourist in. I write in my daily calendar each place that I travel to, the names of RV parks or campgrounds where I stay and interesting things that I do. I also make a note of the temperature, so that when I consider going back to that location, I can see if it was too hot or too cold and perhaps go a different time of year the next time.

I also feel the need to take pictures of places where I go. It is extremely fun to look back at pictures of places that I have been because it triggers the memories and good feelings that I had at the time. This way when I go back thru an area, I can be reminded of what I like and might want to do again.

I also keep a log of how much I spend on gas and camp site fees as well as propane and maintenance/repair items. Keeping the spending journal tells me how much my combined gas and camp fees are. Surprisingly the combined amount has been less than what I spent for rent at my last apartment. Win win for me.

The spending journal also shows me where I can reduce spending if I get into a financial bind and need to lower spending for a few months. Gas and site fees are variables that can be adjusted by just not driving or finding cheaper places to camp, so these can be adjusted downward for a few months if needed.

I find I spend more in the summer months when I am covering a lot of ground traveling far and wide. Summer is really my heavy wandering time, as there are so many places that are best seen in the warm summer months. I am more likely to travel cross country at this time.

My expenses are a lot less in the winter, when I am staying put in one place for longer periods of time, which for me is 14 days at the most. The winter months are when I may get more rest, relaxation and recharging done. It is also the time when I might do some clearing out of old items that I no longer use and replacing some linens or dishes with something new.

Going between these two opposites is a nice balance for me. It is a pleasant cycle of going on adventures during the long days of summer and having periods of rest during the shorter days of winter.

How To Prepare For Travel Days

After enjoying your RV or campground site, on your last evening there, the excitement starts to build about traveling the next day to the next destination. There are a few preparations to make before you go. I like to get everything ready the day before, so that I can get up early and leave without any stress.

Fill up the fresh water tank, dump the black and grey tanks, and put away lawn chairs and other personal items. Walk around the RV and do a visual inspection; check for bulges on tires, make sure storage doors are locked and secure, make sure water and tank caps are secure and just see if anything looks out of place. Also check your oil or other fluids and perhaps clean the windshield for a clear view while driving.

On the inside, put away all items that won't be needed in the morning. Once you wake up and are ready to start the engine, make sure door cabinets are securely closed, loose items are stored and vents and windows are closed as needed. Some people find it easier to have a pre-drive checklist, especially in the beginning, when things are still new.

This is also a good time to mention that heavy items like water jugs or a box of books might be better stowed low for weight distribution, and lighter items like clothes and bedding can be stored higher up. I personally store glass items such as cooking oil and vinegar in a box on the kitchen floor. This is a precaution because occasionally a kitchen cabinet can come open while going down the road, especially a bumpy dirt road, things will be jarred loose. Anything breakable will do better in a box on the floor or in the kitchen sink.

On travel days, also known as moving days, I find it easier to start early in the morning. I like to take my time, stop often, and arrive somewhere in early afternoon. As a general rule, I plan on a 2 to 3 hour drive time. If GPS says it will take 2 hours, I know that it will take me 3 hours. I like to stop at vista look out points and other points of interest along the way. After all, for me it is about the journey, not just the destination.

I like to get where I'm going before 3 pm in the afternoon. Especially in the winter months, when I know it will be getting dark by 5pm. This way I am not trying to back the RV into a tight spot after dark. Also this allows for any roadside mishaps that may delay my arrival time.

I try to check the weather apps to see what the wind speed will be along my route. I find that earlier in the day, the wind is calmer, whereas later in the day, especially in the southwest, the wind can really pick up after noon or 1pm. Be prepared and plan accordingly.

How To Decide Where To Travel; So Many Choices

Styles of Camping; Minimal to Luxury and Ways to Save Money on Camping Fees

Once I have decided my destination, I also think about all of the places to see along the way. It might take me 2 weeks or 3 months to travel to a destination 500 miles away, depending on what I want to see, do and experience along the way.

I myself have done all the different types of planning, from no plan at all to making plans and reservations months in advance. The first year I started out making no plans or a very minimal idea of what direction I was heading in and potential places to stay along the way. The first year out I was trying to do mostly boondocking, which requires no reservation. I loved those boondocking days and reflect upon them fondly. I stayed in a lot of beautiful, peaceful spots in the desert and in the mountains.

My second year, I wanted to experience a wide variety of camping styles. So, I stayed at very fancy RV resorts and very minimal style campgrounds and everything in between. I discovered a wide variety of all different kinds of places to stay and a huge range of prices. I found out that although I like the RV resorts with pools and hot tubs and mini golf and the occasional on site restaurant, I also equally love the secluded mountain dry camping with a beautiful dark sky to view the stars. I continue to try different places and get all the different experiences. Remember I'm all about getting the experiences.

I have found my Passport America camping membership to be of good use during this time, as there were several nights when I was able to get 50% off my stay. I also did the New Mexico State Annual Camping Pass for $235, which allowed me to stay at State Parks in New Mexico for no additional cost, with no hook-ups, or $4 per night if I wanted electricity. Most of New Mexico is at an elevation of 4,000 to 5,000 feet, so this was a good option for summer and fall, although a lot of the state parks are in remote areas with no cell service.

    I continue to do all styles of camping. I love having the different experiences and each place that I go has its good points and bad points. I like to focus on the good and appreciate it. I have an attitude of gratitude because I get to experience this lifestyle every day.

Styles of Camping: RV Resorts, Campgrounds, Boondocking

There are many different styles of camping. Some people prefer going out into the desert or forest and finding a secluded spot to boondock or dry camp with no hookups and no neighbors. Others might enjoy a campground where there are no hookups and plenty of room between neighbors, or a campground with hookups and fairly close neighbors as well as a swimming pool. While other folks enjoy an RV resort, where there is a swimming pool, hot tub, hot showers, laundry facilities and a lot of close neighbors.

I would suggest that you try every style of camping to find what you like best. And even the most diehard boondockers will occasionally find themselves in an RV park to empty their tanks, do laundry and take a long hot shower.

Keep in mind that some campgrounds charge extra for a variety of things such as: 50 amp service, extra vehicles, more than 2 or 4 people to a campsite, etc. Some campgrounds charge for electric when paying at the weekly or monthly rate. Always check the details so that you are not surprised by additional charges.

Some campground or RV parks have a no pet policy or limit the number of pets you can have. Others might not want to have RVers if their vehicle is more than 10 years old. As each place is independently owned, the owners and managers have total control over who they allow to stay at their property. Don't be offended by this, just move on to your next option.

Campground Memberships

There are many types of camping membership available. Some are extremely cheap and others are extremely expensive.

If you find yourself eventually living in your RV full-time, you may get to the point where you prefer having an electric hookup and find yourself in RV resorts or campgrounds that offer hook-ups.

Passport America is probably the most popular camping membership, as it is very affordable at around $35 a year. This allows you 50% off select campground daily rates. The only down side is that there may not be a campground in the area you are going to. Also, some parks limit the discount to 1 or 2 nights and most don't accept the discount during the height of their season. This might include a warm place in winter or a cool place in summer, or if you are in a tourist town, don't expect the discount.

Escapees, Good Sam and KOA offer a 10% discount at some select RV resorts and campgrounds. This can be a decent option and over the weeks, that 10% can add up to a large savings.

New Mexico State Park Annual Campground pass is around $235 for non-residents. This lets you stay at several state campground during the year. There is no additional cost to stay at a campsite with no hook-ups and only $4 a night if you are at a site with electric hook-up. The only downside is that a lot of their parks are in locations with no cell signal. So, if you need cell service for work or streaming TV, do your research.

Then there are the more expensive memberships such as Thousand Trails and many camping resorts affiliated with Coast to Coast RV Resorts.

Thousand Trails can be $500 to $800 a year. When considering Thousand Trails, go to their website to see where their parks are located, as they don't have them in every state and there may not be any where you plan to camp. Keep in mind that some parks charge a small nightly fee for 50 amp service to cover the additional electric usage.

You may want to go visit a few of their parks before considering this option as some people have commented that the parks that they visited are not up to their personal high standards. Although plenty of other RVers have commented that they love the Thousand Trials parks they have visited and that it makes full time RV living affordable for them.

All About How to Be Successful At Boondocking

Finding a Good Boondocking Location

The term boondocking is used when an RVer can find a place to park overnight or for a few weeks, in a spot that is free. Usually there will be no hookups and no place to dump the tanks or trash. The first rule of boondocking is to leave the area as you found it. Pack it in and pack it out.

Finding a free spot can be tricky, but gets easier with experience. If you are on the road and just need a place to park for one night there is usually some easy options, such as a store parking lot or City Park. Some popular favorites are; Casinos, Walmart, Cracker Barrel, Home Depot and Menards. However, always check with the manager of the store first. Also be aware that increasingly more cities are enforcing their city ordinance where there is a ban on people sleeping in their RVs.

Other longer term boondocking places where you may stay up to 14 days is Federal land, such as Bureau of Land Management (BLM) and state and local parks and other government land.

There are several free apps that you can download to your smart phone which can help you to find a location. However, keep in mind, that even though a site may be listed on the app, things could change for an individual site making it no longer allowed for overnight camping. It is always advised to check with the local manager or ranger and beware of signs indicating if camping is allowed or not and if there is a fee.

Do You Need Solar To Boondock

When boondocking, some people find it easier to use solar panels to run their electric devices, some RVers will run their generators, but this can be noisy and too loud for neighbors when running the generator for several hours.

My first year of living and traveling in my RV, I tried to find mostly boondocking sites. The biggest reason was just to see how cheaply I could live this lifestyle. I wanted to be prepared in case my finances took a nose dive and I had to live cheaply. I found it somewhat easy to put out my solar panel and collect enough energy in my portable battery to run my laptop and devices. I also found it very easy to conserve water and take the occasional shower at the local gym or do a quick sink bath.

You don't have to have solar to boondock, but if you can afford one 100 watt panel and one little solar generator, you might find it very helpful.

Conserving Water When Boondocking

When boondocking, it is important to keep in mind the size of your fresh water tank and how long you want that water to last. Finding ways to use a minimal amount of water is essential when boondocking.

For washing hands, the use of wet wipes does the job and is very handy. Walmart has a jumbo size package for around $5 which can last me 2 months. When living in a house, I would wash my hands a LOT. I find I use the wipes several times a day and still feel just as clean. Of course after handling raw meat I will wash with hot water and soap.

Some people use the wipes instead of a daily shower. However, I find what works best for me is a simple bowl bath or sink bath. I can wash my hair using this method as well when boondocking. I also have a nationwide gym membership which gives me access to showers, although the main purpose of the gym membership is to keep up with general fitness and muscle strengthening. Some truck stops offer showers for a fee. I have never done this, but I have heard the price can be $5 to $12 or free if you use a gas rewards card. Also paying the daily entrance fee to some county or state parks give you access to showers.

I keep 2 squirt bottles, bought from the dollar store. One has fresh water and the other has a vinegar water solution. These can be used to rinse hands and dishes, to keep water usage to a minimum. When using the sink, put the water on the smallest trickle amount you can. The squirt bottle comes in handy when brushing my teeth, as I don't want to use water from the tank. You would be surprised at how little water you actually need.

When washing dishes, use paper towels to clean the food and grime off dishes as much as possible before washing. Never let food or grime go down the drain as it will clog your grey tank or at least get grime on your sensors so that they give a false full reading.

Some people use the 3 dish pan method for cleaning dishes, which is hot soapy water in the first pan to wash. The second pan has water from the fresh water tank to rinse and the final pan has boiled or filtered water for a final rinse.

You can also wash your dishes with a squirt bottle containing 1/4 white vinegar and 3/4s water and use a few paper towels. This is most helpful when boondocking and running low on water. The vinegar will kill germs and get rid of grease. The use of paper plates to eat on and plastic sandwich bags for leftovers will help reduce the amount of dishes there are to wash. But this is a personal preference and some people prefer plastic or glass dishes.

Where to Get Water, Dump Tanks and Trash While Boondocking

Some towns may have a gas station that offers dump stations for emptying the grey and black tanks, for free or a small charge. In some states there are free dump stations at roadside rest areas or even at waste water treatment plants. Some RV parks will allow you to use their dump station for a small fee and fill up your water tank.

I found what works best for me when dealing with trash, is to use the small grocery bags, as they fit easily into a small trash bin from the dollar store. This bins fits in the bathroom quite easily, where I can close the door so there is no smell. The small bags are easy to find a place to dispose of them, such as gas stations and stores that have trash collection bins in their parking lots. I can leave one at the gas station when buying gas and one at the grocery store when buying groceries and one at Cracker Barrel when buying dinner, etc.

The number one thing that bothered me while boondocking and had me driving into town was the trash piling up. It seems I could not go more than 5 to 7 days before it was driving me crazy and I had to get rid of it. If not for the trash, I could easily boondock more than 21 days before needing to dump my tanks or get water and groceries. Of course, there were times that I would move within days, to another location just to experience a new location.

SECTION SEVEN

Budget and Expense

Budget

Many people who are contemplating going full time in their RV have concerns about how much it will cost. The answer is that it will vary depending on the person. Most spending, such as groceries, eating out, and entertainment will be about the same as living in a house. RV insurance and health insurance will vary depending on your situation and your residence address.

The big variables are camp site fees and gas for the RV. Most RVs will be get 5 to 12 miles per gallon, maybe a little more for a van style RV. So the amount you spend on gas will vary depending on how often you travel and how far you go. If you stay in one spot for 2 weeks and move 200 miles to your next spot or if you stay in one spot for 5 days and travel 600 miles to your next spot, gas consumption will vary. You can see how this will greatly impact your monthly gas amount. If gas is $3 a gallon and you get 10 mpg, then it will cost about $120 to drive 400 miles.

Camp site fees vary greatly as well. If you are in a tourist spot at the height of the season, you will be paying $45 to $165 dollars a night or $300 or more weekly rate. If you are in the middle of nowhere and off season, you may get something for $20 a night or $300 a month. And there are plenty of people who boondock and don't pay anything for camp fees.

Budgets will vary greatly but here are a few things to consider in your budget:

RV payment

Collision insurance, Road side service insurance and health insurance

Cell phone/ internet/ TV/ Netflix streaming fee

Campsite fees

Camping memberships like Escapees and Passport America

Gasoline

Propane

Maintenance/repairs

Food; buying groceries and eating out

Entertainments; tourist stops, museums, shopping

My Actual Expenses for 3 Years

These expenses are;

7 month average for June thru December 2017.

12 month average for January thru December of 2018

12 month average for January thru December 2019

Monthly Average:

	2017	2018	2019
Collision/roadside insurance	$102	$102	$102
RV registration and smog test	$25	$25	$25
Mailbox service	$24	$36	$39
Phone Apps	$5	$7	$10
Cell service phone and tablet	$131	$131	$131
Netflix/Hulu	$20	$20	$20
Camping Memberships	$16	$16	$16
Propane	$18	$11	$11
Maintenance/repairs	$39	$120	$76
Campsite fees	$278	$493	$262
Gasoline	$271	$319	$346
Total Monthly	**$929**	**$1,280**	**$1,038**

Food and entertainment was not tracked so I have no idea what I spend. I would guess maybe $600 a month. Health insurance was not included as that is a big variable for people. RV payment was not included as that will vary as well or can be zero.

As you can see, campsite fees and gasoline was my two largest expenses. I have put about 36,000 miles on the RV in 3 years. This is very low as some RVers cover this many miles every year.

My campsite fees are relatively low due to my using camping memberships and getting good discounts with them; Escapees, Good Sam and Passport America are my favorites. I also stayed at a lot of campgrounds that were free or very low cost, such as State Parks, Bureau of Land Management (BLM) campgrounds and boondocking.

The maintenance and repairs over 3 years covers oil changes and RV washes, 2 new tires, a new windshield, a new toilet, and fridge components.

My Current Situation with Expenses

As you can see, my current expenses are about $1,038 a month plus groceries, eating out, entertainment and health insurance. This is far cheaper than my monthly housing expense living in a house. Compare $608 for campsite fees and gas versus over $1,400 for rent and utilities or over $1,800 for mortgage and utilities.

This is how I have been able to prepare for retirement the last several years. This is also how I am able to be in retirement for the current time.

Will I ever move back into a house? Maybe, but I don't have a crystal ball to see the future. I am empowered by knowing that I have the knowledge and the tools to live as cheap as possible for as long as necessary or as long as I want.

SECTION EIGHT

Travel Log

Grand Canyon South Rim, One of My Favorites

For my first travel share, I thought it appropriate to talk about one of my favorite places in the US; the Grand Canyon. I have visited the south rim many times and I never get tired of it. The views from the rim are spectacular. There are endless places to pull over in the RV and take in the view.

The Grand Canyon is 277 miles long and at some points 18 miles wide and more than a mile deep. A lot of that is National Park and National Forest and other parts are included in various Native American Reservations.

The National Park has set up a great visitor experience at the south rim. During the solar eclipse of August 21, 2017 I was sitting in a great spot on the south rim to experience the eclipse. It was a very memorable day, and still one of my favorites from my RV travels.

Typically I drive up through Williams, Arizona, a historical Route 66 stop, where I might get a milk shake and fill up the gas tank. It is about 50 miles to the south rim from there. If you want to stop and stretch your legs along the way, you can visit the little road side attraction that looks like Flintstone village. I think it was like $5 to get in. Sometimes I drive straight thru to Tusayan, Arizona. This little town offers gas, groceries, restaurants, hotels and places to camp. 2 miles north is the gate to the canyon where you pay a small entrance fee.

Once inside the National Park there are many places to park for the day, such as the Visitor Center and the grocery store. The park offers hotels, campgrounds, grocery store and many restaurant options. I was surprised to find that many of the restaurants had good food and at a reasonable price. My favorite restaurant is at Bright Angel Lodge. The free bus system is hop on hop off and will take you to many places along the rim.

You can spend 2 or 3 days going to all of the different look-out stops offered on the bus route. There are also lots of places around the rim that you can drive to. I really enjoyed hiking along the south rim for many miles. When hiking, be sure to take your water bottle and wear appropriate shoes.

If you find yourself near northern Arizona, you might want to add this to your list. But note that Williams and the Grand Canyon are at high elevations of about 6,700 feet and therefore you can expect cold and snow if you go during the winter months.

Great History in Los Alamos, New Mexico

While passing thru New Mexico I stopped at the little town of Los Alamos, famous for its history of being a top secret military base during World War II. Watch the series "Manhattan" on Hulu and you'll see the history of this place. This is where several top level scientist worked for years to create the first nuclear weapons and worked on the top secret weapon called the Manhattan Project.

First of all, the views of the mountains from this little town are just spectacular. There is a great museum with lots of photos and historical notes. Although most of the base is gone, there are still a few of the original homes that housed some of the top level scientist. It is all very cool and interesting.

Upon approaching the town you can stop at the Main Gate and get a feel for what the base occupants went thru back in the 1940s. The town offers hotels, restaurants, parks and a library. It is definitely worth taking a day to stroll thru and get a feel for what life was like on the base 75 years ago.

When you're done at the base, you can drive over to Bandelier National Park and camp among the beautiful trees.

Aliens in Roswell, New Mexico and Hiking Carlsbad Caverns

While making the rounds thru New Mexico, I just had to stop in Roswell. As a kid, I read the books on aliens and have always had a fascination with all things UFO related. Well, anything paranormal or weird also. Roswell is a great little town. The museum is very interesting and has some fun things to look at. They even have a UFO that lights up periodically and it is surrounded by aliens. I really got a kick out of that.

I spent the night at Bottomless Lake State park near Roswell, which is beautiful and quite. This is a good place to just relax and recharge. The next day I headed south to visit Carlsbad Caverns. The elevator was not working while I was there, so I hiked down the entrance of more than a mile. Going down was not too bad, but walking back up an incline of a mile was tough, but well worth it. The walk thru the caverns is simply awesome and I am so glad I made the hike.

The cave is home to thousands of bats which come out about an hour before sunset. They stop letting people go down about 2 or 3 hours before dark, so that it is empty of people when the bats come out. So, plan accordingly. I stayed to watch the bats come out, standing outside in the parking lot. I was not able to see them, but maybe I was too far away. Next time, I'll sit in the viewing area provided. Safe travels everyone!

For more travel log, journey stories, and remote working ideas, check out my blog at RemoteChris.com.

About the Author

Chris Conley grew up in the Ohio Valley region of the Midwest and spent more than 25 years of her adult life in the Northeast Florida coastal area, working a full time corporate job. She has worked exclusively from home, aka remote, since 2011.

At the age of 48 she spent a few years living in different areas of the US and then settled in southeast Nevada for the next four years. After age 50, she began traveling as much as possible and has been to several other countries, and most of the US states including Alaska and Hawaii.

She spent more than 3 years doing extensive research on the RV lifestyle before buying an RV. In early 2017 she moved into her RV full-time while working remote and traveling the US. In early 2019, at the age of 55, she retired from corporate life and continues her RV adventures. She currently is self employed working remote from her RV while traveling the US and living full-time in her Class C Motorhome.

Contact Info

Follow the Blog at:

http://RemoteChris.com/

Follow RemoteChris on Facebook:

https://www.facebook.com/RemoteChris

email: Chris@RemoteChris.com

See Remote Chris's unique designs on Funny T-shirts and Cool Coffee Mugs at:

https://WhizzyShop.com/

Etsy: https://www.etsy.com/shop/WhizzyShop

Teespring: https://teespring.com/stores/WhizzyShop

Amazon: https://www.amazon.com/s?k=WhizzyShop&ref=nb_sb_noss_1

Social Media for WhizzyShop

Facebook: https://www.facebook.com/WhizzyShop/

Instagram: https://www.instagram.com/whizzyshop/

Twitter: https://twitter.com/WhizzyShop

Pinterest: https://www.pinterest.com/whizzyshop/

Made in United States
Orlando, FL
08 June 2023